The Best Monologues of the 80s (Women)

SOLO!

The Best Monologues of the 80s (Women)

Edited by
Michael Earley and Philippa Keil

APPLAUSE
THEATRE BOOK PUBLISHERS

SOLO! The Best Monologues of the 80s (Women)
Copyright © 1987 by Applause Theatre Book Publishers
Acting Solo and *Your Sixty Seconds of Fame* copyright © 1987
by Michael Earley

The Acknowledgements pages constitute an extension of this copyright
page.

Library of Congress Cataloging in Publication Data

Solo!: the best monologues of the 80's (women).

(The Applause acting series)
Summary: Presents a collection of powerful monologues for actresses, written by the decade's most influential and popular dramatists
from the United States and Great Britain.
1. Monologues. 2. Acting. 3. Actresses. 4. American drama—20th
century. 5. English drama—20th century. [1. Monologues. 2. Acting.
3. American drama—20th century. 4. English drama—20th century.]
I. Earley, Michael. II. Keil, Philippa. III. Series.
PN2080.S66 1987 812'.045'09 87-17475
ISBN 0-936839-66-x (pbk.)

Applause Theatre Book Publishers
211 West 71 Street, New York, NY 10023
(212) 595-4735

All rights reserved. Printed in the U.S.A.

Applause Theatre Book Publishers
406 Vale Road
Tonbridge, KENT TN9 1XR
Phone: 0732 770219 Fax: 0732 770219

Fourth Applause Printing 1994

ACKNOWLEDGEMENTS

Grateful acknowledgement is made for permission to reprint excerpts from copyrighted material:

AGNES OF GOD by John Pielmeier. Copyright © Courage Productions, Inc., 1978 and 1982. Reprinted by permission of the author.

ALBUM by David Rimmer. Copyright © as an unpublished dramatic composition by David Rimmer, 1980. Copyright © David Rimmer, 1981. Reprinted by permission of the author.

ALL SHE CARES ABOUT IS THE YANKEES by John Ford Noonan. Copyright © 1987 by John Ford Noonan. Reprinted by permission of the author.

ALL KIDDING ASIDE by Charles R. Johnson. Copyright © Charles R. Johnson, 1985. Reprinted by permission of the author's agent, Agency for the Performing Arts, Inc., 888 Seventh Avenue, New York, NY 10106.

AS IS by William M. Hoffman. Copyright © William M. Hoffman, 1985. Reprinted by permission of Random House, Inc., 201 West 50th Street, New York, NY 10022.

AUNT DAN AND LEMON by Wallace Shawn. Copyright © Wallace Shawn, 1985. Reprinted by permission of Grove Press, Inc., 920 Broadway, New York, NY 10010.

BIRTH ON A HARD SHOULDER by Howard Barker, from TWO PLAYS FOR THE RIGHT by Howard Barker. Copyright © Howard Barker, 1982. Reprinted by permission of Riverrun Press, Inc., 1170 Broadway, New York, NY 10024.

BLOOD MOON by Nicholas Kazan. Copyright © Nicholas Kazan, 1984. Reprinted by permission of the author's agent, Agency for the Performing Arts 888 Seventh Avenue, New York, NY 10106.

BODIES by James Saunders. Copyright © James Saunders, 1979. Reprinted by permission of the author. All rights whatsoever in this play are strictly reserved

CONTENTS

INTRODUCTION: ACTING SOLO

Where playwright and actor meet on the most matched and even of terms is in the monologue. The monologue is a shared moment between the playwright and his medium, the actor. It provides an opportunity for both artists to collaborate more directly than at any other stage of the theatrical process. With the monologue, the actor and playwright create a theatre of their own. Even the dialogue portions of a play are more collaborations between actor and actor, or actor and director. The playwright becomes a third or fourth party. But in the monologue the playwright depends entirely on the actor for clarity and precision. And for the actor, these gifts of extended thought and speech can be the key to liberation; points of separation that leave other actors in the play behind and propel the solo actor above everyone else in our estimation and concern. So totally are actor and playwright fused in the monologue, so completely intertwined, that the spirit and voice of one becomes indistinct from the other. The result can be that unique harmony rarely achieved on any stage.

The best theatrical monologues have a kind of thrust and propulsion that rivet our focus and attention. They grab an audience, stop time, and suddenly make the actor/character's plight the sole intention of the play. Good monologues leave behind the common language of the play and take on more exalted qualities. They take the speaker to a higher orbit of performance. When we speak of a Sam Shepard monologue, for instance, we frequently use the word "aria" (airs). In the theatre of the past, "hearing" and watching great actors grapple with and tame the language of great dramatists was the single reason for going to the theatre.

In a sense, monologues are exhibitions of writer's and actor's courage. They are blatant expressions of will, purpose, thought, feeling, rage, confusion, irony, hilarity, regret, defeat, and dozens of other human emotions. They are also egocentric in the extreme. A really fine monologue pinpoints a character's quirks and longings. Oftentimes it unleashes something raging inside the character. It may not, and should not, give a whole meaning to a play (only the *total* play can do that), but it can give luminous meaning to a single moment onstage. Just for a passing instance, maybe a minute or

1

more, a character is given concentrated definition and content; perhaps more than we have yet experienced. Actors love monologues for their freedom and focus. They are showpieces and showstoppers. They jar us into understanding what a character has been straining to say. Often they are a test by which we can measure an actor. More often they separate the good writers from the bad. And after the play is said and done, monologues leave us with a memory of the event. Usually they contain the lines we most remember.

But just what is a monologue? Obviously it is a speech in which one person talks solo to himself, another character, or the audience. They provide the moments when the public spectacle of drama abruptly becomes personal and intimate. In the writing of a gifted playwright and the mouth of a daring performer, the monologue rises to the same plane as the operatic aria or any other tour de force of solo performance. It can also be as gutsy as a "rap" or bit of pop singing. But without the actor to give it release, the inner dynamic of a monologue remains uniformly contained and clumped on the page. Like music, every monologue is written like a score, with its own rhythms, beats, crescendos, and climaxes. And as with any sustained piece of showmanship onstage, monologues leave an unforgettable imprint on an audience when perfectly executed. We may not remember much about the dialogue in the scenes of Shakespeare's *Hamlet,* but we all remember details about how an actor performed any of the soliloquies that begin "To be or not to be," "O what a rogue and peasant slave am I," and "Now I am alone."

Contemporary monologues, like Shakespeare's great soliloquies, all have their roots in ancient song, odes, orations, and the extended speeches in Greek tragedy. That's how the form developed in the West. They equally find their source in prayer. Once the Greek actor Thespis stepped out of the chorus to deliver his speeches solo, the art of individual acting was born. And at that point, too, the actor's detachment from the background gave us something onstage to heighten our attention and curiosity.

Monologues are also playwright's tricks, providing actors with ingenious ways of attracting and holding our attention. They can also lead to moments of pure indulgence, or just be a pack of lies. Who said that a monologue has to tell the truth? Yet it is the actor's job to give the monologue a *sense of truth* or, at least, illustrate it with a convincing performance strategy so that a constellation of words will do their trick and have their effect. Playwrights who love the sound of their own voices, Shaw for one, stud their plays with monologue after monologue. Most other playwrights use them more sparingly, and even tentatively, too frightened, perhaps, to hear their own voices or too certain that they will give away the essential meaning of their play. For monologues are confessions. They startle us with their candor, which is why they are so hard to do well. A character speaks urgently, and we, invariably, remember what he or she has said. And we remember it for a long time.

Just as they function like uninterrupted pieces of music or orations, monologues can also be like poems. They entrap a play's lyricism and challenge an actor in the skillful use of words and phrasing. Any decent monologue, just like any poem, can stand on its own as a piece of handsome writing. It still needs a speaker, though, to give it a final dimension. Yet monologues— contemporary ones, especially—can also be halting and stumbling; not things of great beauty at all. They can capture a character's inarticulateness as he or she strains to find the words, struggles to fill the void. Samuel Beckett writes only monologues nowadays to give his characters' obsessive thoughts free range onstage. Peppered with pauses, lapses, repetitions, and silences, contemporary monologues isolate the human inability to use words and make them meaningful. They hint at moments of modern experience where language no longer has the full expressive power and resonance to re-create the world in all its dimensions. Some monologues hope that a string of jangled phrases and "you know what I means?" will do the work of full thoughts and sentences. The speeches in David Rabe's *Hurlyburly* are severely stuck in this condition.

Monologues can also be excessively coarse and violently profane. They can catch an urban pulse that communicates largely through vulgarity. Some of the speeches of David Mamet and Eric Overmyer take us into a world of language that has a vicious core. In explosive pockets of the world, like South Africa, where discord is the rule rather than the exception, playwrights reproduce chaos and tension in the language of their rage. Even when the violence is more latent and fundamentally political and social, such British playwrights as David Hare, Howard Barker, Howard Brenton,

David Edgar, Jim Cartwright, and even Harold Pinter fight despair in monologues that characterize the personality and source of evil.

Monologues can also be highly physical as well as verbal. Some of the best have an intuitive feel for the way words can communicate through an actor's body as well as his voice. Steven Berkoff, for example, knows that actors speak to us *physically* as well as verbally; the body functions onstage in concert with the mind. And even more than male playwrights, women dramatists, like Nell Dunn, Sarah Daniels, Debbie Horsfield, Timberlake Wertenbaker, and Sharman Macdonald, can find the subject of their speeches in female physicality. The body, and thoughts of the body, can be uncommonly expressive. For the actor, these kinds of monologues can lead to rare moments of solo performance. Tom Stoppard's speeches show the actor that monologues can also be acrobatic, and that humor, at its very best, is physical and like a verbal pratfall. For some writers, words and sentences can be amorous, distilling, as Sam Shepard does in *Fool for Love* or Christopher Hampton does in *Les Liasons Dangereuses,* the intensity and jealously of sexual love.

During the past decade, the monologue has taken on new meaning and function. The well-crafted confessional speech, like those in the plays of August Wilson, are certainly still with us. But we seem to live more and more in a time where dialogue—really talking and listening *to* each other—is quickly being replaced by the monologue and a talking *at* one another. Wallace Shawn's plays, whether talking with André Gregory in *My Dinner with André,* or talking through the two women in *Aunt Dan and Lemon,* creates the effect of words being spewed at the audience. But we experience this all the time nowadays and are bombarded with examples of it daily: television chat shows, stand-up comics, tell-all autobiographies, political speeches, therapy sessions, protest rallies, advice manuals, T.V. evangelists, disc jockeys, voice overs, sales pitches, publicity spiels, rock videos, "rap" singing, and on and on. Someone is always telling us *their* side of the story rather than the *full* story itself. In fact, hardly anyone seems to know what the story is about anymore.

With the advent of "performance art" in the 1970s and a rebirth in old-fashioned storytelling, the solo performance piece and one-per-

4

son show is now as common as it once was rare. Actors have always trotted out their anthology and "historical" character pieces (i.e., Mark Twain, Charles Dickens, Emily Dickinson, etc.) between other engagements. Now more actors—and younger performers not strictly classifiable as actors, like Laurie Anderson—are using the medium of the solo performance as the setting for a whole evening's work. In the case of Laurie Anderson, her spectacles are a combination of theatre, rock concert, and pop painting. For a performer like Lily Tomlin, the writer Jane Wagner's solo monologues walk a fine line between comic routine and single character dramatizations. In other cases the performer's own autobiography, as in the monologues of Spalding Gray, or observations of show business types and daily encounters with street people, such as the monologues of Eric Bogosian, become the stuff of solo theatre.

In a decade when great acting onstage has become a true rarity (a generality more true in the United States than in Great Britain), these different kinds of solo performance have now become serious factors in the acting process. Being *oneself* onstage as well as being a *character,* allows the actor a liberation that traditional theatre roles seldom provide. They encourage the actor to be more himself or herself, letting his or her voice penetrate the mask of acting. Since the teachings of Stanislavsky, the modern actor has been laboring hard to transform into someone else. Now both sides of the actor's self are on display. Analogously, reducing the human story to one's own words and gestures, traditionally the function of literature and writers, is now a territory open to anyone. The "new" performer can use his or her own words and not just those of a playwright. Solo acting gives the actor the freedom to truly make material his or her own and to reassert the will to take back possession of the stage.

5

YOUR SIXTY SECONDS OF FAME

Acting alone onstage, especially when faced with a crucial auditioning situation, is all too frequently talked about in terms of fear and terror. But let's look at it in the opposite way, as a kind of joy and exhilaration. Taking center stage puts you right at the heart of the theatrical experience. Rather than being at a disadvantage, you should feel the power of being in complete control. Unless the actor is totally at ease with the prospect of performing, how can you expect anyone watching you to take a keen and genuine interest in what you have to offer? The full enjoyment of acting is infectious and flows effortlessly from the stage out to the audience. This essential joy of performance, apart from the basic anxiety all of us feel at being singled out and "watched," really must be in place before you can attempt to do what follows. The *angst* of acting is the first obstacle you simply must clear from your path.

We assume that actors are looking at *Solo!* in the hope of finding fresh auditioning material, and maybe even some unexpected and new surprises from unfamiliar writers. But how you can best use this material onstage is what we want to explore with you.

Just by leafing through this book you're already accomplishing the first major step: choosing material. But let this choice be guided by something even more fundamental: choose material that best suits your capacity as a person as well as an actor. In other words, find a monologue that is close to you; not something that is close to the actor you would most like to be, but a piece of writing that reflects the actor you are now. In time, conditions will change as you change. But for the moment don't choose something old if you're young, don't toy with something flashy and "hip" if you're not. If you pick something British, for instance, be aware of the context and the *accent*. Are either of these out of your reach or your realm of experience? Many of the British pieces in *Solo!* present few obstacles or difficulties for American actors. We made sure of that in our selection process. Some can even be done with an "American" accent or by simply "translating" British words into American phrases. But remember that all writing, from whatever part of the world, has its own indigenous rhythms which only real familiarity can breed and make work. Honestly knowing your own capacity on this score can help you avoid a critical mistake when it comes to choosing a monologue.

Probably the best rule of thumb we can offer you here is to match your own personal sensibility with that of an individual playwright. Once you've made your choice, the monologue itself should immediately provoke you to search out its complete source, so that you can see and savour the speech in its full context as one part of a complete play. It's simply foolish for an actor to learn a monologue but be completely ignorant of the full text. There are really no shortcuts to good acting. What will you do, for instance, if a director begins asking you in-depth questions about your character or other moments in the play? Go about preparing your monologue just as you would a full role in a complete production. Now that you have one or several monologues in hand, let's plunge right into the deep of this section—the audition.

Auditions, no matter what anyone says, are often won or lost in the *first sixty seconds*. One minute is really all the time you have to truly establish a solid presence and make a definite claim on our attention. The first moment we lay eyes on an actor is rarely forgotten. That may sound prejudiced, but it is, in fact, true. And the sixty second countdown begins as soon as you enter the room, even before you speak your first line. Just your mere "presence" radiates an aura that the spoken monologue will only confirm or contradict. Yet in that first unspoken minute, it can often be "love" or "hate" at first sight. So begin now to think and learn how you can use these seconds to your full advantage.

Any audition is a performance. Make no mistake about that, even though we call them tryouts. And you can think of it as a performance—a solo performance—in which you are the star. The audition is also a very specialized kind of job interview in which you just don't answer questions but *perform* answers. But don't think of it as a contest with other actors. You are really competing with the clock and the short attention span of your auditors; especially short if they have seen a lot of other actors during the same audition. They want to be captivated by someone special, someone who likes the job of acting. Someone who is a professional and won't waste time. Unlike other job interviews, in an audition you rarely get the opportunity to repeat or retract what you just said or did the second before. Those for whom you are performing (director, casting agents, drama school representatives) are clearly looking for talent. But they are also looking for a person with an appetite for work; someone who can become part of an ensemble and withstand the pressure of concentrated effort. Auditions are frequently tense because the eventual rehearsal process is even more intense. Show them, immediately, that you can bear the weight of an opening night performance. They are *not* looking for inadequacies, and they *will not* overlook flaws. But that's perfectly understandable. If they choose you for a part or place, so much time and energy will go into you. So they must get the clear impression from your audition that you can do the job better than anyone else. If you can master and break the sixty second barrier, you can be on the road to fame.

Getting through an audition in the correct frame of mind and with the right stuff requires a process you can repeat time and again. It should be a process no different from any other acting process you would use in rehearsal or performance. Here's one that seems to work best. It is a system that can be expanded to suit larger performance challenges or contracted to meet the concentrated needs of an audition. It incorporates *all* that is most useful from the many different techniques of actor preparation. And it distills what every actor—amateur or professional—needs to know in order to deliver an honest level of performance. Here are ten specific steps, linked in a chain, which can be quickly memorized in sixty seconds:

1. PREPARATION
2. RELAXATION
3. CONCENTRATION
4. COMPENSATION
5. MOTIVATION
6. CHARACTERIZATION
7. PHYSICALIZATION
8. IMPROVISATION
9. REVELATION
10. RESOLUTION

This chain contains all the fundamentals of good acting. It is not some magic chain of gold that will instantly turn you into a great performer. But, if you work through each step properly, it is a

8

system that will not only get you through an audition but through an entire performance. We'll make general comments about each step in the process and then apply it more directly to the audition itself.

1. PREPARATION

No actor can work without being solidly prepared. And our approach here is to put you in the *highest* state of preparation. We'll begin by assuming that you have already chosen your material. Perhaps you've picked one classical monologue and one contemporary. But why not prepare a whole "audition repertoire" of different kinds of material? Being prepared means being able to shift gears from one kind of monologue and mood to another. As an actor you should strive to develop your range and not stay too confined within the narrowness of a couple of favorite pieces. Give your talent the opportunity to grow by experimenting with all kinds of pieces. You'll notice that *Solo!* is an expansive collection of the most varied kinds of monologues. That should be an indication of how we would like to encourage you to look at your acting, in broader terms while still remaining essentially yourself. Preparing a selection of monologues—perhaps six—means that you will never go stale. But proceed at a pace that will allow you to learn and know your material well.

Knowing your material means more than just learning the words and lines. Memorizing is not the challenge in this stage of preparation. Knowing indicates familiarity and intimacy with the play in all its parts. Really *read the play*. Not just once but several times. Investigate its background. Reveal its sources. Decipher its context and content. The best actors, even if just preparing for an audition, will read a script several times. Once you are performing the play, you never stop reading it. Carry the play with you, so that you can read it wherever you are. See it when other actors perform it. You'd better be curious about it because it is now part of your life as a performer. In other words, live and breathe the material. Let it grow on you. You, the character, and the whole play have now formed a partnership. Don't abuse the contract by learning only a single speech.

Further steps in this kind of preparation might be to experience ways that the monologue is written. A good trick is to write or type out the monologue as a means of experiencing the fusion of words and phrases. You might also write out new monologues for your character that the playwright has not written for his own play. The attempt here is to get deeper into the consciousness of the character and the writer. Unless the actor is willing to inhabit and discover the full life and world of his material, the acting of it will always seem false, uninformed, and, at its worst, dreadfully dull. Excite yourself by turning this stage of preparation into an adventure in which you unlock the secrets of the play and expose them.

Now start looking at your chosen speech in detail. What about it surprises you, moves you, makes you laugh? Humor is a powerful ally onstage. It can also be one of your most valuable assets in an audition. It breaks the ice and makes you appealing. Wit is a commodity that the best actors have in abundance. What about odd words and phrases? How can you handle them? What about the strong contrasts between words, the darkness and light that often inhabits the best speeches? Unless you can uncover the hope within the seeming hopelessness of a Beckett speech, for instance, the entire monologue will only result in something dead and dreary. Can you uncover the hope in the speech you've chosen, the way in which the monologue works towards some future success? Really *look* at the speech in order to unravel the playwright's intention so it becomes your character's intention. What are you trying to accomplish and convince us of in what you are saying? How does the monologue build in expectation and arrive at various plateaus or sudden bursts of recognition? All good speeches have some kind of "build," either upwards or downwards, towards a lively or still climax. Perhaps the speech has different kinds of motion. Maybe it rocks, sways, swaggers, stutters, falters, or trips. What does it *physically* feel like to you? Does it make you want to move and use your body in some special way? Then there is the ultimate personal test: Why do you *need* to say this particular speech and why say it now? Does it make you angry? Does it settle some personal score? Does it say something about you?

Long before entering an audition, the process of preparation begins with questions like these. They are the crucial questions that every actor must ask of a speech. So nail them down as you work on any piece of acting material. When you've satisfied yourself with some answers, you're ready to audition.

The audition itself: As we've already said, the audition is basically a job interview in which you act out your answers. It is *not* a life or death struggle in which your whole being and worth is being put to the test. If that was the case, how could you ever think of auditioning? Be a professional and think of the audition as a necessary stage in a professional process. Don't allow yourself to become incapacitated by something that should be enjoyable.

The best kind of preparation for any audition—apart from really knowing your material—is to begin with the thought that you *belong* at this audition. You are not wrong for the part nor are you out of place being here. All of your years of training and preparation have brought you to this point. And because we are approaching the audition not as a competition but as a race against the clock— overcoming the sixty second barrier—none of the usual feelings of embarrassment or inadequacy need to concern you now. Your objective it simply to work hard and get the job done; to show your acting personality to its full advantage in a short space of time. Believe that you will give the best performance of your career. Forget about the past or the future. The time you should be concerned with is only the present. So put all your energy and thought into this moment.

The preparation of any part—and a monologue should be approached as a part—is a highly technical procedure. Recall all the "given circumstances" and have them clearly before you. Key yourself to the moments just before the monologue begins. Who are you? What has just happened? Who are you talking to? In the time leading up to the audition, do a lot of work on the speech and character but then bury it and merge it into a seamless performance. All good acting demands freshness. It must appear as if it is happening for the first time. Think of the audition as your chance to give new birth to a character and speech. What you must strive for in an audition is *focus:* on the character, on the task, on the words. Become fixed and locked into a purpose. You are preparing yourself to launch into a speech because something *burning* needs to be said.

The image you project to others is doubly important when you enter any acting space. You are being judged on looks and bearing, as well as on the quality and delivery of material. Eyes are auditioning you as well as ears. So pay careful attention to the ways you prepare your dress and appearance. What you wear is crucial. Neutral dress might be the rule but coming on in more flamboyant clothes may be to your advantage. Think about the circumstances and particularities of each audition. Is the part sophisticated or "down and dirty"? Will your looks distract from the importance of what you are saying? Will red or black say something more about you than it says about the character? Costume yourself to meet the needs. Even your choice of shoes can say just as much as your monologue. Clothing has a way of speaking. Once you enter an auditioning space, the *total* you is on display. Leave nothing to chance or distraction. Prepare to look and be the part.

2. RELAXATION

No actor can hope to get the best, physically, from himself or herself without being in top condition. If you've been well trained in proper stage technique and physical work, you probably already know the best means to relaxation. The anxiety of an audition, the anxieties of life, produce tensions. They are the actor's greatest enemies. But muscular tension, especially around the neck and shoulders and in the voice, can be freed and relaxed through a proper physical warm-up. But begin it at home, working on all parts of the body. Adopt a good voice and speech warm-up, particularly if you are delivering a taxing speech or will be expected to sing. And always be prepared to sing. Carry a complicated poem with you to test your vowels and consonants, your sibilants and aspirants. If you have repeated difficulties with speech, seek out a good speech teacher. *How* we say things onstage is as important as *what* we say. Any relaxation techniques should really become part of your daily regimen. Once you get to an audition, you can quickly perform exercises that will tone you for the challenge ahead.

The audition itself: Arriving at an audition early, rather than just on time, can prove to be relaxing in and of itself. When you arrive out of breath, you arrive out of control. But set out from home assuming that the wait will be long and tedious. It usually is. Even assume that the room will be stuffy and claustrophobic. They usually are. Drink juice rather than stimulants in order to flush yourself out. Walk past the deli and donut shop. The taste of coffee or a

12

Coke will be that much better once the audition is over. Caffeine and sugar does strange things to us when we're already in a state of excitement. No alcohol and no drugs. Your mission is to be in complete control over all your functions. The mind needs to be composed and alert in order to give the best performance of your life.

Get an instant warm-up down to ten minutes or less. Some of this can even be done on the way to an audition; perhaps a brisk walk outside where you can talk or sing out loud without anyone paying too much attention. Always try to get out of transportation a few blocks away so that you don't have to plunge into the audition right off the street. Move at your own pace so that you can establish your own personal rhythm. And maintain it throughout the audition.

If the situation doesn't allow for a full warm-up, try doing one in your chair. Create a "state of relaxation" by visualizing the positive benefits of physical exercise: the movement of muscles, the circulation of the blood, the clearing of the head, the deep breathing. Listen and focus on sounds, smells, objects, and faces. In other words, center yourself. Do all you can to *separate* yourself from the tensions inside you. Take along something to read that will make you laugh. Don't listen to a Walkman if it will be just too distracting. Condition your passive self to begin shifting gears into an active mode. If you are just sitting there waiting, do some deep breathing: exhale the everyday self that is you and inhale the self that is you in the role. It's a simple technique. Part of your relaxation should be to find positive ways to fill the time until you are called. But relaxation also prepares you for the next crucial step of concentration.

3. CONCENTRATION

No one can tell you how to do this step easily. Each of us needs to acquire our own means of concentration. There are just too many ways—both practical and spiritual—of centering and focusing concentration on any given task. Being relaxed and conditioned is a good start. Emptying out the mind of its daily worries and strife, so that only the role and the monologue remains, is another good start. Rather than avoiding the task of auditioning, confront it. Make it a joy, an adventure. Maybe you will be "discovered" today. Maybe

13

you will become famous. Since acting means *doing,* remember that there is nothing passive about it. It suggests conflict. So that might offer a good means of focus. Not the conflict and argument you may have had at home with a lover, but the character's conflict. All of your own fears and doubts can be centered on those of your character. So let the character absorb whatever outside conflict may be inhibiting you. Maybe the character wants to be as successful as you. Maybe he or she wants to be famous as well.

A positive way to begin concentrating on your way to an audition is to focus on a favorite play or film, reconstructing all the events in sequence, watching all your favorite actors going through their paces. Make yourself one of them. Become absorbed in your world, the world of the theatre. Many actors lose concentration on some level because the theatre is not special enough for them or because acting has lost its joy. We all spend too much time worrying about income and bills or the fame that eludes us and not enough time being concerned about the theatre. But once you drop these everyday concerns and begin concentrating on the great performances you've seen or been party to, you suddenly enter the best possible frame of mind for doing theatre. Now concentration turns into an eagerness to perform yourself.

The audition itself: Concentrate on turning fears into fixed purposes: getting prepared to enter the audition space, saying hello, and, most of all, readying yourself to say your first line. The opening of a speech is absolutely crucial. Here is where the clock really begins ticking away the seconds. It is the point of no return. The monologue itself begins to take over and take you along. Establish yourself in these first seconds. Root yourself onstage. Isolate the launch point in the speech and send it out to your listeners. Set-up your performance in advance. Mumble a bit of the speech outside the room before you enter. Let everything else evaporate as you begin concentrating on the character's needs and desires. Think of those first words as hot ignition points that will launch your whole performance into orbit. All of your acting will take-off from that cue.

Also use the time before entering the audition to dwell on motivation, the "whys" and "what ifs" of acting. Be concerned with making your performance new and *as if for the first time.* Even at this late stage of concentration, does anything suddenly surprise you about the speech? Rather than going over the monologue again and again to get the words right, work on it organically by concentrating on the events and circumstances leading up to the speech. Enter the room with energy and purpose. Enter it as a character with something important to say.

Also spend time concentrating on physical aspects and different means of unspoken communication. How can your eyes, head, neck, shoulders, arms, hands, fingers, hips, legs, and feet help with your acting a speech? Concentrate on getting the body to act with the mind in perfect harmony.

4. COMPENSATION

In acting, whether in auditions, rehearsals, or full performances, the unexpected can be a handicap. You must always be prepared to compensate for the things that go wrong. Your partner doesn't show up, the room is locked, your name's not on the list, it is cold, you are late leaving work or arriving. Compensate for all these disadvantages. Turn them into opportunities. The world is not perfect. Something always goes wrong. Compensate. Seek alternatives. Always be prepared, for instance, to sight read an unfamiliar script. Expect that the room for your audition will have shifted to some other place. Adapt to each change in plans. Compensate. The actor who can make adjustments onstage, in the very midst of a performance, is an actor who has learned the lesson of compensation.

The audition itself: Gauge the mood of an audition once you've arrived. Is the whole process running late? Is the atmosphere friendly or hostile? Be alert to the mood, not to gossip or other actors' fears, but to all the realities that might help you in your performance. Make sure that the space meets your needs. Are props there for you to use? Is there a sturdy table and chair? How resourceful will you need to be if none of these are available? Compensate for anything that is lacking. With the seconds ticking away, don't waste time searching for help. Size up difficulties in advance and maintain your control over the situation. Master any calamity. Do without something if you must. Allow yourself a well-defined but *constricted* acting circle. Don't expect to use the whole room. Never let events throw you off and distract you from your concentration. Keep apologies to yourself. Above all else, when things go wrong—and they will—don't make excuses. Simply adjust, compensate, and push ahead.

Adjust all your acting to the circumstances at hand. Don't pre-plan and pre-play a speech as if it will we done in duplicate conditions each time. Enjoy any variation that arises. Show that you are a resourceful actor who can perform anywhere. Your willingness to adjust and compensate adds dimension and range to your abilities as a performer. And your resourcefulness is certain to impress a director. This is exactly the kind of actor every director looks for.

5. MOTIVATION

Without doubt, motivation is the single most important link in this chain. Why? Because motivation gives directional focus to all acting onstage. Motivation gives us the *reasons* for doing and saying something through performance. It makes us perform an action or say a speech. Unless the actor knows *why* he or she sits in a specific chair, *why* we are talking to another character, *why* we are taking a drink, or *why* we are saying a speech, any task of acting will only be vague. Motivations provide us with answers.

Acting *without* motivation is dead-end acting. We come onstage to complete a series of choices we have already made in our mind. Motivation provides us with the reasoning and clarity of purpose to turn those choices into active responses. What can any actor *do,* what can any actor *say* with conviction unless backed by the push of motivation?

Motivation is the essential spring that triggers an actor into a scene, a role, a speech. Only after you have asked yourself the essential questions of acting—questions whose answers uncover motivation—can you begin to perform with authenticity: Who am I? What do I want? Where am I going? What obstacles stand in my way? Who am I talking to? What am I seeking or saying, beat by beat, word by word? Until the actor begins providing solid answers to these kinds of questions, acting will only be wasted energy. Point your acting in a specific direction.

The audition itself: Good motivation brings all the goals in a scene or speech together into one clear challenge. It gives the actor the *right* to claim the stage, even if it's just for the few precious minutes that constitutes an auditioning monologue. Conviction comes from motivation. And your auditors will want to see you express conviction and belief from the first second you open your mouth. Once you have settled into your opening moment, you must let the *will*, *needs*, and *desires* of your character totally absorb you. Think of motivation as a replacement for self-consciousness. It is, after all, the consciousness of the character that should now be in control. The character's tasks and words now fill up the time. Your goals will be more easily accomplished if you have found the reason to be onstage.

Giving yourself even the slightest task to perform onstage has a way of obliterating self-consciousness. Walking across the stage trying to solve a mathematical problem puts you at more ease than just walking aimlessly across the room. The mind has nothing to focus on so it dwells on itself. For an audition monologue, isolate a *single* task that will give your acting the motivational push it needs. Find that one key activity that will give all the words clarity and purpose. Once absorbed in the activity, you'll barely even notice the time flying.

6. CHARACTERIZATION

Entering the world of a character is a lengthy and prolonged process. It means trying many different tacts before settling on the right one for you. The actor dives into the character repeatedly in the hope of penetrating all the layers. This is a rich process of discovery for the actor and is never arrived at instantly. You search the character's, as well as your own, personal history to find that equality that suits you both. And you never go public with this private work until a good part of the character's life and anatomy is in place.

For the purposes of an audition, entering a character's world begins from the moment you awake on audition day. How does he or she wash, choose clothes, dress, and groom for the day? What does he or she eat and drink? How do you begin shedding your own habits and take on those of your character? You *and* the character begin living and doing things together. Maybe you *both* choose to wear that red scarf or those brown shoes. Perhaps each of these pieces of dress give you important objects that will help you realize the character in performance. Perhaps you'll want to prepare your hair differently today. Will that help you get to the character? In other words, what will help you arrive at the audition *in character*?

The audition itself: When choosing audition monologues, you might try and search for pieces that demonstrate similarities. Can you, for instance, find something in Shakespeare's Ophelia that is like a character from a contemporary play? These don't have to be similarities that will make two monologues seem redundant, but parallels that are personal ones for you and help you transform from one piece to another while maintaining a strong and steady sense of character. The similarities might even be outrageous and secret ones. No one has to know except you. But transforming from a character in one monologue into that of another can be a peril. So why not try to find characters, or even speeches, that present you with some kind of harmony? You will be judged on your ability to fuse with a character. So your ability to believe in a character and make your audience share that belief is central to all acting. Simplify your audition task with a cast of sympathetic characters who are extensions of yourself. It will really pay off in the end and show in your performances.

The substance and shading that you give your characters will also be carefully noted. Perhaps you can find and add a different element to your role in each audition. Never be afraid to keep working on character. There is always something new to discover. This kind of process protects your characterization from becoming stale and lifeless. What new inflection can you add to a speech? What new turn on a phrase? Try to avoid too much consistency. It has a way of leeching the excitement out of a performance and can usually be detected. Always allow characters to keep surprising you. Treat the audition as you might treat any rehearsal: a new opportunity to go further with a character. But always keep one, solid aspect of character obvious and certain. Always have a strong baseline and never venture too far from it until you are ready.

7. PHYSICALIZATION

You suddenly find that you have a headache, the flu, or a fever. Can the way you feel today help serve your character? As you do your warm-up, you discover you can't rid yourself of a tightness in your chest. Can that be part of the character? The inner integrity of acting must align with how we feel physically. Never divorce one from the other. Any and all physical means must be explored as part of the process of building a role. The outer self is a rich resource that too many actors, especially in auditions, abandon. We rely too heavily on the words of a text. Remember that acting is something that has to be read from a distance. And our impression of an actor registers *externally* at first.

Acting is disciplined, hard work. It demands stamina along with mental concentration. It requires gesture as well as verbal agility. And the two must work in concert. The eyes, for instance, are remarkably important as instruments in a performance. How can they benefit you in your performance? Keeping your body alive and interesting onstage should receive as much work as the way you deliver a speech. If you are pliant, physically, a director will instantly see that he can work with you.

The audition itself: Don't just enter a room, enter it with interest. Make yourself the center of attention. Come in with a strong attitude and disposition. All of you is on trial. All of you is there to be read.

When delivering a monologue, what physical reactions do the words provoke? Too many actors forget to *move* with their words. And a speech that can physically show you off is usually the best kind to perform in an audition. Always pick a monologue that will make you perform an action. But also be careful about excessive gestures like flapping arms and hands that slice the air too much. Suit action to word, as Hamlet says to the players. Stay in control of each movement and gesture, letting the words lead you to a result rather than the other way around.

Voice and speech patterns are also aspects of the physical. Think about the cadence of your speech. Can you find a rhythm in the lines, even if they are not set in verse, that will give the words a musicality? Maybe you might even experiment with singing a monologue, or linking it with some form of music. The effort in an audition is to express a speech with impact. All stage language has the capacity for lively expression. Words can be like objects tossed out to the audience. So projecting the words, as if they had solid weight, will enhance your delivery. Think, too, about the space in which you are performing. How much projection do you need to make your acting real? Project just to your auditors and not to a full house. Keep every aspect of your physicalization within proper bounds.

8. IMPROVISATION

Few actors improvise very well on their own. It takes enormous courage, daring, and self-regard to improvise with truth and conviction and then incorporate it into a full performance. Actors will too often hide behind a playwright's words rather than let their acting come out from behind the words. Yet we all admire creative risks onstage. Rehearsals usually offer ample time to experiment through improvisation. But what about within the confining limits of an audition?

The audition itself: Some auditions may ask you to improvise as a means of exploring your creative temperament. A director may want to explore different aspects of your capacity as an actor. An audition, for the brave, can be approached as an opportunity to take some sudden risks. A moment of improvisation, within the course of a monologue, may yield benefits. Most actors, however, will guard against going off the course of a routine once it has been set. Yet let yourself be taken by a creative impulse if it should suddenly happen.

Dull and consistent acting can hamper you. Our best acting ideas sometimes come to us in the heat of performance, once an audience has reacted to something we have just said or done. Here is a moment you can build upon. If you are in full control of yourself, your character, and your speech, you might think about enlarging on your performance in the midst of an audition. Any actor's job in these instances is to stand out and make an indelible impression. Literal interpretations of a speech have little to do with real acting. Theatricalizing yourself can be a real challenge. Avoiding the prosaic and the mundane can sometimes propel us to make these creative leaps. But do so only if the speech and your confidence naturally lends itself to this kind of risk.

9. REVELATION

Every good monologue contains a crucial moment when the whole speech reveals its intention. Find that moment so you can sustain it in performance. It may come at the beginning, middle, or end of the speech. A moment of revelation can be prepared for and scored. What, for instance, is the kernel of the speech, its most important word or phrase? Maybe it's the most important moment of the whole play. Such a revealed moment is something you can build a whole performance around.

The audition itself: Flatly delivered monologues, lacking a build, suggest flat acting. All dramatic language plunges us into a search for something. Yielding revealed moments in a monologue is really what an audition is all about. If you can transform an audition into a public search for something, that vital incident in the monologue, it will add impact to your task. Your concentration will increase, your physicalization will engage with the search, and your characterization will lock in place. You will also find yourself becoming one with the playwright's intention. Your struggle then becomes the center of our attention. That kind of involvement and discovery onstage is what your auditors will be looking for.

Find the right thread or through-line that will lead you to a revelation. Don't *rush* towards a result but *build* towards one. Use the words of the speech to heighten excitement and expectation. And when you make your discovery, make certain that it registers. Never smother the impact of a monologue's revelation. Sometimes they clearly stand out in a speech surrounded by pauses. They are there for the taking. Other times you have to work to find it. Revelations give speeches and performances the satisfaction of having arrived someplace important. Make sure that you can properly chart the path to one in your performance.

10. RESOLUTION

We all know that any kind of ending is hard to produce well. And any actor runs the risk of arriving at a result much too early. In monologues we have to give thought to how we end them and clearly signal that the performance is over and resolved. Any piece of acting is never over until there is a final curtain. Never just stop a performance. End it with finality and a conclusion.

The audition itself: Find the *curtain* in any monologue. Each speech has one. Is is fast or slow, a fadeout or a blackout? How long of a hold do you need? What is the best way to signal that you are through performing? Just as you build the opening of your audition carefully, so should you carefully prepare its conclusion. It can lead to success or ruin. The same rules for a fully staged performance apply to the audition. Letting the seconds of your ending subside, also gives you the moments to prepare for your next monologue. Your resolution lets you round off a performance. Perhaps more than any other part of acting, it shows your ability to control material and yourself. And throughout the minutes of an audition, control and completeness is what you strive to achieve.

AGNES OF GOD   John Pielmeier

A psychiatrist's office. DR. MARTHA LIVINGSTONE *(40s), a court-appointed psychiatrist, has been examining a young nun,* SISTER AGNES, *accused of mysteriously giving birth to a child and then murdering it.* MARTHA LIVINGSTONE *reflects on* HER *own past and loss of faith.* MARIE, HER *sister and also a nun, had died from neglect in a convent.*

DOCTOR: Oh, we would get into terrible arguments, my mother and I. Once, when I was twelve or thirteen, I told her that God was a moronic fairy tale—I think I'd spent an entire night putting those words together—and she said, "How dare you talk that way to me," as if *SHE* were the slandered party. And shortly after Marie died, I became engaged for a very short time to a romantic Frenchman whom my mother despised, and whom consequently I adored. We screamed ourselves hoarse many a night over that man. (SHE *laughs)* And you know, I haven't thought of him in years. I haven't seen him since I left him—no, *pardonnez-moi,* Maurice, since *he* left me. What finally happened was that I . . . well, I . . . I was pregnant and I didn't exactly see myself as a . . . well as my mother. Maurice *did,* so . . . *(silence)* And then once, in Mama's last years when she was not altogether lucid, I told her in a burst of anger that God was dead, and do you know what she did? She got down on her knees and prayed for His soul. God love her. I wish we atheists had a set of words that meant as much as those three do. Oh, I was never a devout Catholic—my doubts about the faith began when I was six—but when Marie died I walked away from religion as fast as my mind would take me. Mama never forgave me. And I never forgave the Church. But I learned to live with my anger, forget it even . . . until *she* walked into my office, and every time I saw her after that first lovely moment, I became more and more . . . entranced.

23

ALBUM   David Rimmer

*October 1963. Here are two monologues spoken by the same
character at different points in the play.* TRISH *(14) is lying on*
HER *bed, having a girl-talk with* HER *best friend* PEGGY. TRISH
is anxious that HER *infatuation with singer* BRIAN WILSON *of*
THE BEACH BOYS *has destroyed* HER *interest in boys* HER *own
age.* SHE *fantasizes about walking on the beach with* BRIAN
WILSON. *The second monologue takes place August 1965.*
TRISH *(now 16) has switched allegiance to* THE BEATLES. SHE
is sprawled on HER *bedroom floor, holding a picture of* JOHN
LENNON. SHE *has turned defiant with the new music and mood.*

TRISH: It's always right before I go to sleep. I take my radio
from under the pillow, and I put it away, and I lie there and close
my eyes. . . Sorta like dreaming but I'm away too. . . We're
walking on the beach, me and Brian, not holding hands or anything,
just walking. The sun's going down over the ocean, there's nobody
else there, you can hear the waves. Then we stop, right at the edge,
I look at his face, and I know he's gonna touch me, I can feel it, like
a fire. I look at the sky behind him and I can see the stars, I can
count them, it's not even dark. Then he says, "Listen. . ." And I
close my eyes, and I hear the ocean, and I feel it inside me, tingling,
and warm, and I can't wait for him to touch me . . . The beach is
in California. Can you imagine? The Pacific Ocean. . . I can't
even think of it, it's so far. Think we'll ever get to go there, Peg?
I'd give anything to go. . . .

* * *

TRISH: *Okay! Okay! (SHE grudgingly turns down the radio,
and the volume of "Ticket to Ride" goes down.* SHE *gets up, mut-
tering and grumbling as* SHE *walks around the room in frustration)*
Haven't you gone yet? . . . God. . . *(SHE looks out the window and hears the sound of a car starting up and pulling away.*

24

SHE *yells) I'll listen as loud as I want! (Afraid* SHE *said it too loud,* SHE *takes a quick look outside, then, relieved, goes to her radio, and turns it back up.* SHE *sings along with the second verse of the song, changing the lyrics to show her anger toward her parents: from "She" and "me" to "I" and "you." As* SHE *sings,* SHE *takes out her mother's picture album and a pen, and pack of cigarettes with matches and ashtray—all hidden under the bed.* SHE *sits on the floor and defiantly lights a cigarette. After a second or two of pleasure, the smoke gets in her eyes and* SHE *reacts in pain. Then* SHE *turns her attention to the album, leafing through it, writing in it, turning down the radio a bit)* Writin' in your sacred old picture album again, Mom. "A Thousand Stars," "Surfer Girl," Ecch. Ancient history. *(Smiles)* "Eight Days A Week," "Help!" "Ticket to Ride." Here's what happens, Mom: I meet John Lennon at a party and he needs help just like a regular person, he's having problems with Cynthia and he's just waiting for the right bird to fly away with and I'm it and we run away together and leave you and your old album behind. And he's my Ticket to Ride. . . *(SHE kisses the picture of John on the lips; then gets up)* Sick. Gotta stop fallin' in love with pictures. *(Looks out the window)* C'mon, get dark. *(The sound of a car pulling into the driveway scares her.* SHE *fans the air for smoke, hides the cigarettes, runs to the window)* Shit! Back already? Can't you give my any peace—? *(Yelps in delight)* Peggy! *(Looks closer)* Barb? And a guy—? *(SHE runs out the door as the radio plays.)*

25

ALL SHE CARES ABOUT IS THE YANKEES
John Ford Noonan

The present. A New York City apartment. MAUREEN *(39) has not left* HER *apartment in 43 days.* SHE *has been obsessively following* HER *favorite baseball team, the Yankees, during the season on TV. Here* SHE *tapes a letter to* HER *father in Minnesota explaining* HER *predicament.* HER *friend* SPANKY *looks on.*

MAUREEN: Gee, Dad, how have you been? . . . I'm sorry I haven't written in over two months, but I've been so busy. I hardly get to bed and . . . and CLANG, CLANG, CLANG goes my alarm clock. Time to face another exciting New York day. For me everything's been so great, I don't know where to start . . . Where do I start? . . . I'm still as popular with the boys as I was back in Chisolm. Just listen!

(SPANKY *suddenly bangs table to simulate* "LOUD KNOCKING")

Another one trying to knock down the door! All joking aside, I've got a great new job doing . . . actually they're still deciding exactly—

(Long silence)

Dad, the reason I haven't written in over two-plus months is that I haven't been able to leave my room. You ask why? Well, one day I just couldn't get to the door. It's been forty-three days, Dad, I don't want you to worry. Fifty-six days is my limit. If I'm still stuck here after that long, I've got a real clear plan for what happens next.

(Suddenly singing opening line of Buffy St. Marie song)

"YOU'RE NOT A DREAM, YOU'RE NOT AN ANGEL, YOU'RE A MAN"

(Laughing, closing eyes)

Now there's one you mostly liked . . . Every time I close my eyes and send my mind back to Chisolm, all I see is you rocking on the porch. Every June we'd pull it down from the loft out in the barn and lug it up on the porch. The winter would've made the squeak even worse so I'd squeeze some "3-in-1" on all the joints. You'd try it first and then I'd sit on your lap. I'd purr, "Dada, the squeak's still there." You'd laugh and say back, "Give us something everyday to get our talking started." God, did we go on and on. Remember when I was eleven what you told me about sentences: ". . . that all the great sentences that still hadn't been used were floating just above our heads and that if we kept reaching up as hard as we could, we'd sooner or later grab the one we needed." Dada, your little baby still believes in sentences. Never before has she reached any harder.

Dad, you were pretty close to a perfect father.

(Laughing)

You're the only one I can't be angry at. That's about the one clear thing of the last forty-three days. Every day I get more angry. Every day I add more names to the list. Dad, I've got this list I spend most of my mornings on. It's called *THE OBERFELD REVENGE LIST*. It's based on my carefully computed quotient of "Oberfeld Hate and Rage." There are five columns I put the people in. Column one is "worth murdering." Column Two is "worth maiming." Three is "worth causing a crippling injury." Four is "worth causing serious but temporary damage." Five is "worth ruining their week." Many people move from column to column according to how I feel from day to day. Mom's never moved. She's always been "worth murdering." Right now I'm angrier at her than when she was here. At least once a day I want to rip off her arm and beat her head in with it. So much for lists.

(Forced good cheer)

Anyway, here's my plan at the end of fifty-six days. I'm coming home to Chisolm. Dada, I'm heading West to be with you. I don't know how I'll get that knob turned but I will. Somehow I'll get down to the lobby and out the door. Hail a cab out to JFK. In the air. Land in Minneapolis and hop on that bus north. Once I get on that bus north, watch out. You and I are going to spend hours and hours rocking away and going over just about everything. I think that's what you have to do sometimes: go all the way back to where the trouble started and see where it was you veered off. Dada, your baby started veering off the day I left you and mom at the Minneapolis Airport. The person I was faded pretty fast only not a lot came to take her place. New York City's great if you've got a vicious reason for being here . . . but if you're just sorta here looking for what it is you might like to try, *WATCH OUT!* I've got a real good friend named Brian who makes all my dolls and he describes my problem as follows . . .

("Doing BRIAN's voice)

Kid, you're an 80-watt bulb and New York's a thousand-watt socket. Every time you plug in, you blow out!" Dad, that's all I am: 39 years of sorta looking for what it is I might like to try. Was what I lacked already in my eyes when I came out of Mom? Or maybe was it something like a fog that came over me at 12 or 15? Once I'm settled a few days into Chisolm, it's something we can go over! I'd really like to know when you started to worry? Was I ever tested for anything and found lacking? Was there ever some game even at three or four that I truly loved to play? Would you call me a child with a clear sense of life? A look of purpose? Did I ever possess any deep drives? If so, when did they leave me? As a baby was I fun to play with? Did I smile a lot? Did I already . . . Was I even then . . . Were . . .

(Can't go on, takes breath, does go on)

Going back even farther, was a I baby you and mom wanted? Planned for? Hugged each other over late into the night? Did you ever once make a list of a few of the things you dreamed I might become? How many times did you wish I never was? How often did I pull crap that made you want to kill me? Were you ever truly proud of anything I did? When I led the girls' basketball team to the county title, were you ecstatic? Embarrassed? Jealous? All three? Did you enjoy watching me move around the court? To your eye was my jumpshot a thing of rare beauty? What about my ass? Did my buns make you wonder? Did my tits make you gasp? Was it you or mom who went with me to confront Coach Johnson because I always refused a bra under my uniform? I kept explaining I couldn't get full extension on my jumper wearing one but Johnson kept insisting I was out to tease guys? Tease guys?!! All I had my on mind was going to the hoop. I remember I was crying after. Did you hug me? Did you want to and couldn't? I know these are the kinds of questions you hate to hear, but when you're stuck like I am, it's often . . . sometimes I . . .

(Can't go on. Takes breath, does go on)

One thing I'd like you to do the minute you get this letter is write back real quick and tell me how Alicia Carmody's doing. I got a letter from her last Christmas about moving back to Chisolm and how she loved finding everything so much the same. She said what she had run away from was what she really wanted all along . . . Anyway, she mentioned in her last paragraph about seeing you out back of the Hubert Humphrey Junior High doing jumps with Rusty. Dada, can Rusty still jump like he used to? Do you still clean his stall all by yourself? Does riding bring you a peace that is like nothing else? Does living in Chisolm make you feel like you have a place where you belong? I sometimes think I've never had a place in my life where I truly belong and feel at home. Talking to you like this and I'm already half way there . . . I'm watching you read this sitting on the john. Remember how the mail used to come and how you'd go read it on the john, locking the door behind. Are you crying? Do I hear some sobs? . . . To say goodby I'll sing you your favorite.

(SPANKY sings)

"TEA FOR TWO AND TWO FOR TEA
ME FOR YOU AND YOU FOR ME"

(Can't remember next lines of verse.
Repeats opening two but again no more)
Love, Dada, . . . from your only child and favorite daughter.
(SPANKY presses STOP button, removes tape, lays gently on
table. Silence.)

ALL KIDDING ASIDE   Charles R. Johnson

The present. A New York apartment. SCOTTY (20s), an aspiring
comic, practices HER routine in the bathroom. This speech opens
the play and introduces HER to the audience.

SCOTTY: Are you ready? If you're not, I can come back.
You seem like a really tame bunch. So polite. Like you just came
from a Nancy Davis film festival. Ever stop and thing that if Reagan
had not gone into politics, he and Nancy would probably be doing
guest shots on *Loveboat*. Yes . . . with Van Johnson and June
Allyson. Oh my god, I just had a gruesome thought. What if Van
Johnson and June Allyson were in the white house? Makes your
flesh crawl, doesn't it? Sorry I didn't mean to get us off on such a
down start here tonight. *(Pause)*

Welcome to the show. My name is Scotty Devlin. I know what
you're all thinking . . . How come she has a boy's name? Actually my real name is Heidi. But I had to change it when I lost my
virginity. Everyone named Heidi must change their name when they
lose their virginity. That's the rule. Look at these three girls over
here all rustling through their programs. You're all Heidis, right?
Sorry. Am I embarrassed or what. My luck, Van and June are
here. *(Pause)*

Actually, I lied to you. Scotty is my real name. You see, when
I was born the doctor was either far-sighted or a prankster, because
as I popped out, I remember it vividly, he declared "It's a boy." In
fact, I was a boy until my mother changed my diapers for the first

time. Can you imagine their surprise. My mother fainted. My father just stared, "He can't be my boy." I was in stitches. *(Pause)*

They tried calling me Judy for a while but I just wouldn't respond. Would you have? There's a Heidi nodding her head. Oh, by the way, the part about all Heidis having to change their names when they lose their virginity, I didn't lie about that. That is a known fact. *(Pause)*

Yes, it's true. Think about it. How many grown women do you know named Heidi? All the Heidis I know are about 8 years old with long blond braids down their backs. They all wear pink dirndls with little white aprons. And are surrounded by goats. They skip their way into high school, getting A's in Home Ec. Then one day, probably on their 21st birthday—wham—Veronica, Yvonne, Desiree. *(Pause)*

This is absolutely true, I promise you. You've never heard of a child being called Yvonne, have you? If I had been called Judy, I'd have to change my name when I stopped wearing bangs. Have you ever met a seventy year old woman named Judy? It sounds like she should be chewing gum and skipping rope. *(A beat)*

I'm not making this up. Right before middle age sets in, Cindys become Harriet, or Beatrice, they have that option. All Wendys die at puberty. Regretable, but necessary. I sort of like being called Scotty, besides it's better than my middle name—Doug. *(Pause)*

Look, I gotta run. But before I go, I just want to say that I hope all the guys who are sitting here tonight with a girl named Heidi, wake up tomorrow morning with a Desiree.

31

AS IS   William M. Hoffman

*The present. A New York City hospital for AIDS patients. A
HOSPICE WORKER, a dowdy middle-aged volunteer, wearing a
dark dress and bright lipstick and nail polish, opens the play with
this speech to the audience. A black humorist, SHE approaches
HER part-time "sainthood" with a heavy dose of sarcasm and irony.*

HOSPICE WORKER: Mother Superior always used to say,
"Watch out for the religious cranks, Sister Veronica." When I started working for the hospice I had a touch of the crank about me. I
think maybe that's why they gave me the old heave-ho from the
convent. But I've kept my vow of chastity and I've made a
pilgrimage to Lourdes.

My job is to ease the way for those who are dying. I've done
this for the last couple of years. I work mainly here at St. Vin-
cent's. During the day I have a boring secretarial job, which is how
I support my career as a saint.

I was much more idealistic when I started. I had just left the
convent. I guess I thought working with the dying would give me
spiritual gold stars. I thought I'd be able to impart my great wisdom
to those in need of improvement. I wanted to bear witness to dramatic deathbed conversions, see shafts of light emanating from
heaven, multicolored auras hovering above the heads of those in the
process of expiring. I always imagined they would go out express-
ing their gratitude for all I had done.

A quick joke: Did you hear about the man who lost his left
side? . . . He's all *right* now. All right now. *(SHE laughs)* We
tell a lot of jokes in my line of work.

32

AUNT DAN AND LEMON   Wallace Shawn

1971. Summertime in Oxford, England. A little house filled with a child's toys and furniture. DANIELLE (AUNT DAN) *(40s), a dogmatic and eccentric American, who is a tutor at Oxford University, has developed a close and intense friendship with the impressionable and sickly* LEMON, *daughter of* DAN's *friends.* AUNT DAN's *long stories and seductive opions entrance* LEMON. *In the first monologue,* AUNT DAN *tells* LEMON *about* GEOFFREY, *one of* HER *lovers. In the second monologue, the time has shifted to the present.* LEMON *(now 25) sits in an armchair, still frail and sickly.* SHE *recalls wanting to run away to* AUNT DAN *and also recounts one of* DAN's *more unlikely obsessions,* HENRY KISSINGER.

AUNT DAN *(to* LEMON*):* You see, the thing was, Geoffrey was the most fantastic liar—I mean he was so astonishingly handsome, with those gorgeous eyes and those thick, black eyebrows—he just had to look at a woman, with those eyes of his, and she immediately believed every word that he said. And he didn't mind lying to his wife at all, because she'd trapped him into the marriage in the first place, in the most disgusting way, and she just lived off his money, you know—she just lay in bed all day long in a pink housecoat, talking on the telephone and reading magazines and ordering the servants around like slaves. But he knew she'd go mad if he left for the week, so he went to her looking totally tragic, and he said, "Sadie, I've *got* to go to Paris for a conference for at least three days, and I'm so upset, I just hate to leave you, but some professors over there are attacking my theories, and if I don't defend myself my entire reputation will be just destroyed." So she cried and wailed—she was just like a baby—and he promised to bring her lots of presents—and the next thing was, I heard a little knock on my tiny door, and in came Geoffrey into my basement room. I mean, you can't imagine—this tiny room with nothing in it except all my

33

laundry hanging out to dry—and here was this gigantic prince, the most famous professor in the whole university, a great philosopher, coming to see me, a starving second-year student who was living on a diet of brown bread and fruit and occasionally cheese. Well, for the first two days we didn't *move* from bed—I mean, we occasionally reached across to the table and grabbed a pear or an apple or something—and then on the third day we called a taxi, and we went all the way into London to this extraordinary shop—I'd never seen anything like it in my life—and while the taxi waited we simply filled basket after basket with all this incredible food—I mean outrageous things like hams from Virginia and asparagus from Brussels and paté from France and olives and caviar and boxes of marrons glacés, and then we just piled it all into the taxi, along with bottles and bottles of wine and champagne, and back we went to my tiny basement and spent the rest of the week just living like pigs.

* * *

LEMON: Naturally, at that time, I often used to dream about running away from my parents and going to live with Aunt Dan in London, and I must admit I often pictured that Kissinger would be dropping in on us fairly regularly there. At least, I imagined, he would never think of missing Sunday breadkfast, Aun Dan's favorite meal. For Kissinger, I imagined, she'd always prepare something very special, like some little tarts, or eggs done up with brandy and cream. And Kissinger, I felt, would be at his very most relaxed around Aunt Dan. He would stretch himself out on the big couch with a sleepy sort of smile on his face, and he and Aunt Dan would gossip like teenagers, both of them saying outrageous things and trying their best to shock each other. As for myself, the truth was that I was quite prepared to serve Kissinger as his personal slave—I imagined he liked young girls as slaves. Well, he could have his pleasure with me, I'd decided long ago, if the occasion ever arose. Few formalities would need to be observed—he didn't have

34

the time, and I knew that very well. An exchange of looks, then right to bed—that would be fine with me. It wasn't how I planned to live as a general rule, but for Kissinger, I thought, I would make an exception. He served humanity. I would serve him. *(Pause)* But a lot of people didn't feel about Kissinger the way we did, and after a while we realized something that we both found rather surprising. As it turned out, one of the people who didn't like Kissinger was actually Mother! In fact, Mother didn't like him even at all—just not one bit—and throughout that summer, when Mother and Aunt Dan would chat in the garden in the afternoons, whenever the conversation turned to the subject of Kissinger, as it often did—and more and *more* often, it seemed to me—things would suddenly become extremely tense. And, naturally, at the time I wasn't in a position to see these conversations as steps toward a final split between Mother and Aunt Dan, but that, of course, was exactly what they were.

BIRTH ON A HARD SHOULDER
Howard Barker

The present. An abandoned tuberculosis hospital. ERICA (20s) a down-and-out drifter, has taken refuge in one of the wards. SHE is talking with FINNEY, a former stockbroker, who, unable to contemplate the future under a recently elected Socialist government, has killed his entire family. Quizzing him about the graphic details, SHE launches into a speech about HER own view of the value of life.

ERICA: I used to keep hamsters as a kid. When one died or got trod on, my dad bought me another one. So I got to know a lot of hamsters. And they were all different. Some built good nests, some built lousy ones. Some could climb up the curtains and some could hardly climb at all. And some bit you and some didn't. They were all individuals. They were like human beings. Every one was different. And yet there I was, treading on 'em. And I knew that what was true of hamsters had to be true of rats as well. Every rat that ever lived was *unique*—amd *every ant! (Pause)* You have to keep it in perspective. The fact that we are different doesn't make us valuable. There's too much fuss about this precious fucking *human life. (Pause. FINNEY is horrified)* You should talk to Hilary. She's good on that. She says—hold it—hold it—'Respect for human life is the rock on which they built the status quo.' Got it! *(SHE* grins. *Pause)* First time I've got that. Do you love language? I do. Though Hilary's got a thing about that. She says it's—fuck it—no, it's gone . . . Somethin' anyway. Did you want a cocoa? *(He just stares)* You should talk more. *(SHE turns. Goes a little way, stops. Inspired)* 'The sledgehammer of social conformity!' Or conformism, is it? That's it, anyway. *(He doesn't react) Language. (SHE carries on her way)* Cocoas in the operating theatre. *(SHE grins)* It really was. Lung tissue in all the teacups.

BLOOD MOON   Nicholas Kazan

The present. Sunday after Christmas. MANYA 20, *a medical student at Columbia University, is preparing to entertain* ALAN *and* UNCLE GREGORY *for dinner. One year ago* SHE *was raped by* ALAN, *and became pregnant.* SHE *intends to serve him a dish that contains parts of the aborted fetus, which* SHE *had frozen.* MANYA *explains* HER *revenge motive to the audience.*

MANYA: This part is harder for me to reveal. *(Long beat. SHE sighs)* The police. You're probably wondering why I didn't go to them. Sometimes I wonder the same thing. And then I remember the stories. You've heard them. Women who find the police interrogation almost as grueling as the event itself. Women who are disbelieved, mocked. Rape cases seldom go to court and when they do, seldom result in conviction. After all, it'd be my word against his. Besides, I felt sufficiently humiliated, and it'd only make things worse to stand up in court and snivel. "Yes, your honor, he *did* put his dick inside me." *(Long beat; SHE stares at the audience)* Alan injured me in an intensely intimate fashion; I sought an intensely intimate response. *(SHE seems to be finished. SHE spreads the tablecloth and sets out a stack of plates plus silverware, wineglasses, four double candelabras, a loaf of bread, etc. This done, SHE turns back toward the audience)* What disturbs me now, in retrospect, is what the following events suggest about me ... and about—for want of a less pretentious term—the state of my soul. Was I being excessive? Masochistic? Was there something else I might have done which would have been truly noble rather than perpetuating this cycle, this circle, of perversity? Sometimes I think so. At other times, I reflect on this and I glow with pride. *(Resumes setting the table)* Yes. Sometimes, despite the horror—or because of it ... this all seems perfect.

BODIES   James Saunders

The present. A suburban livingroom in London. ANNE (40's), a housewife, opens the play with this speech to the audience. SHE reflects on the lack of romance in HER life and HER husband MERVYN's repeated infidelities.

ANNE: I was never, thank God, an Idealist; no romantic; the dewy-eyed approach irritated me. I suppose the parents contributed, with their talk of love and niceness, their comfy-cosiness, covering a shoddy making-do with each other. My first period, I thought: so that's what's behind it all—*this* discomfort, *this* mess. And these things sprouting in front, these impositions, to be hiked about, hawked about through life in case I should happen to breed. The nerve! Pretty brash cynicism; but better that way than the other.

Useful too, a good defence, it gave me an edge, I used it when the time came, when the occasion warranted. "I'm having a period, do you mind!" They minded , mostly; well, at that age. Another trick I had, toffees in the handbag; faced with an importunate male at the end of a dreary evening he thought I should pay for, I'd pop a Sharp's Kreemy into my mouth and start chewing. That spiked the romantic gun, at the expense of a filling or two. Or both together, the ultimate deterrent. *(SHE talks as if chewing toffee)* "I'm having a period, do you mind!" I grew out of it, of course, matured; I mean I learned to enjoy myself, take what was available, including *romance,* why not; feet on the ground, though, head below the clouds. I thought I was unfoolable, set for life. My expectations were never more than reasonable, before and after marriage; I anticipated difficulties, and got them; I coped. His first infidelity—though I didn't believe in the concept—I pushed out of sight, refusing to be disturbed. And the others. And then, well into what I thought was my maturity, coming up forty would you believe, the cataclysm. The mess. The mess of it. I was not unhappy, that was the point, not dissatisfied as far as I knew, there were no great blisses but what do you expect, I expected nothing more; and then, out of nowhere, the first intimations: a restlessness, a strange unease, like the feeling you have before you know you're going to be sick. I increased my activity, became rather manic, threw a big party; I hated to be alone, doing nothing; time was going by so quickly, suddenly, *had* gone by, forty years of it, probably more than I had left. My time was running out, I had to use it, mark it with my brand. Something in me started looking for a meaning, a value that would give meaning, to make it all right that I was getting older and would die, die and lose everything. Be lost.

BRIGHTON BEACH MEMOIRS   Neil Simon

September 1937. Evening. A house in Brighton Beach, Brooklyn.
BLANCHE *(38), a nervy, asthmatic widow who lives with* HER
sister, KATE, *and* HER *family, has had to bear a long day of frus-*
trations. The last strain of the day is HER *daughter,* NORA, *who*
wants to move out of the house and pursue a career on Broadway.
NORA *accuses* BLANCHE *of not loving her.*

BLANCHE: My God, Nora . . . is that what you think of me?
[NORA. Is it any worse than what you think of me?]
BLANCHE: *(hesitates, trying to recover)* . . . I'm not going to
let you hurt me, Nora. I'm not going to let you tell me that I don't
love you or that I haven't tried to give you as much as I gave Laurie . . . God knows I'm not perfect because enough angry people
in this house told me so tonight . . . But I am *not* going to be a
doormat for all the frustrations and unhappiness that you or Aunt
Kate or anyone else wants to lay at my feet . . . I did *not* create
this Universe. I do *not* decide who lives and dies, or who's rich or
poor or who feels loved and who feels deprived. If you feel cheated
that I had a husband who died at thirty-six. And if you keep on
feeling that way, you'll end up like me . . . with something much
worse than loneliness or helplessness and that's self-pity. Believe
me, there is no leg that's twisted or bent that is more crippling than a
human being who thrives on his own misfortunes . . . I am sorry,
Nora, that you feel unloved and I will do everything I can to change
it except apologize for it. I am tired of apologizing. After a while it
becomes your life' work and it doesn't bring any money into the
house . . . If it's taken you pain and Aunt Kate's anger to get me
to start living again, then God will give me the strength to make it up
to you, but I will *not* go back to being that frightened, helpless
woman that *I* created! . . . I've already buried someone I love.
Now its time to bury someone I hate.

THE COLORED MUSEUM   George C. Wolfe

NORMAL JEAN REYNOLDS, *a black country girl from the South, sits with a large white egg between* HER *legs. Throughout the monologue* SHE *hums to it like a mother to a newborn baby.* SHE *claims to have laid it. But other things have happened to* NORMAL *as well. And* SHE *tells* HER *story to the audience.*

NORMAL: My mama used to say, God made the exceptional, then God made the special, and when God got bored, he made me. Course she don't say too much of nuthin no more, not since I lay me this egg.

Ya see it all got started when I had me sexual relations with the garbge man. Ooowee did he smell.

No, not bad. NO! He smelled of all the good things folks never shoulda thrown away. His sweat was like cantelope juice. His neck was like a ripe-red strawberry. And the water that fell from his eyes was like a deep, dark, juicy-juicy grape. I tell ya, it was like fuckin a fruit salad, only I didn't spit out the seeds. I kept them here, deep inside. And three days later, my belly commence to swell, real big like.

Well my Mama locked me off in some dark room, refusin to let me see light of day cause "What would the neighbors think." At first I cried a lot, but then I grew used to livin my days in the dark, and my nights in the dark .... *(SHE hums)* And then it wasn't but a week or so later, my mama off at church that I got this hurtin feeling down here. Worse than anything I'd ever known. And I started bleedin, real bad. I mean there was blood everywhere. And the pain had me howlin like a near-dead dog. I tell ya, I was yellin so loud, I couldn't even hear myself. Nooooooo! Noooooo! Carrying on something like that.

And I guess it was just too much for the body to take, cause the next thing I remember . . . is me coming to and there's this big white egg laying 'tween my legs. First I thought somebody musta put it there as some kind of joke. But then I noticed that all 'round this egg were thin lines of blood that I could trace to back between my legs.

(Laughing) Well, when my mama come home from church she just about died. "Normal Jean, what's that thing 'tween your legs? Normal Jean you answer me girl!" It's not a thing Mama. It's an egg. And I laid it.

She tried seperatin me from it, but I wasn't havin it. I stayed in that dark room, huggin, holdin onto it. *(SHE hums)*

And then I heard it. It wasn't anything that coulda been heard round the world, or even in the next room. It was kinda like layin back in the bath tub, ya know, the water just coverin your ears . . . and if you lay real still and listen real close, you can hear the sound of your heart movin the water. You ever done that? Well that's what it sounded like. A heart movin water. And it was happenin' inside here.

Why I'm the only person I know who ever lay themselves an egg before so that makes me special. You hear that Mama? I'm special and so's my egg! And special things supposed to be treated like they matter. That's why everynight I count to it, so it knows nuthin never really ends. And I sing it every song I know so that when it comes out, it's full of all kinds of feelings. And I tell it secrets and laugh with it and . . .

(SHE suddenly stops and puts her ear to the egg and listens intently)

Oh! I don't believe it! I thought I heard . . . yes! *(excited)* Can you hear it? Instead of one heart, there's two. Two little hearts just pattering away.

Boom-boom-boom. Boom-boom-boom. Talkin to each other like old friends. Racin toward the beginnin of their lives.

(Listening) Oh no now there's three . . . four . . . five, six, more hearts than I can count. And they're all alive, beatin out life inside my egg.

(We begin to hear the heartbeats, drums, alive inside NORMAL's *egg)*

Any day now, this egg is gonna crack open and what's gonna come out a be the likes of which nobody has every seen. My babies! And their skin is gonna turn all kinds of shades in the sun and their hair a be growin every which-a-way. And it won't matter and they won't care cause they know they are so rare and so special cause it's not everyday a bunch of babies break outta a white egg and start to live.

And nobody better not try and hurt my babies cause if they do, they gonna have to deal with me.

Yes any day now, this shell's gonna crack and my babies are gonna fly. Fly! Fly!

(SHE laughs at the thought, but then stops and says the word as if it's the most natural thing in the world)

Fly.

COME BACK TO THE 5 & DIME, JIMMY DEAN, JIMMY DEAN   Ed Graczyk

September 1975. The 5 & Dime of a small town in West Texas. MONA (late-30s) is nervous and asthmatic. SHE has kept alive the memory (fact or fantasy) of a one-night romance with the legendary actor, JAMES DEAN. MONA worked as an extra in the film GI- ANT, made nearby but back in the 1950s. Convinced that HER son, also named JIMMY DEAN, is the product of that brief union, MONA tells JOE (the child's real father) about that night in 1955.

MONA: That night I laid there is the back seat to the Buick and kept thinkin' about how I was chosen above all them thousands of other . . . starin' out the window at the millions of stars an' the outline of that beautiful house way off the the distance. Suddenly, one of those stars exploded, burst away from all the millions of others an' fell from the sky . . . landin' right behin' the house . . . behin' the front of Reata. I leaned over the seat to point it out to Joe, but he had tramped off somewhere, all mad 'cause he wasn't chosen, too. I pulled my blanket aroun' my shoulders an' started to walk to where the star had fallen to earth. I walked past the front gate down the road to the house. It was so quiet and still . . . the only sound was comin' from a far away train, blowin' its whistle an' chuggin' off into the night. When I got to the front porch, this voice comin' outta nowhere says, "Isn't it a little late to be callin' on your neighbors?" It was him. I knew it. I knew it the first minute I heard his voice. Then he said, "Don't just stand there bein' unfriendly. Come on up on the porch an' sit a spell." As I moved up the stairs, I reminded him that I was the one who gave him a match that mornin' . . . an he thanked me again. We spent that whole entire night togclher . . . the sun started to peek out from over the edge of the earth, turnin' the sky into the brightest red I ever saw.

[JOE. *Mona, what are you sayin'?!*]

MONA: *(Sharply to* JOE.*)* We walked together to the gate an' he thanked me for sharin' the night with him an' then we both walked away in separate directions.

THE CONDUCT OF LIFE   Maria Irene Fornes

The Present. A Latin American country. OLIMPIA *(30s-40s), a servant/housekeeper to the wife of an army officer, gets frustrated when* HER *mistress tries to force more work on* HER. HER *litany sums up* HER *tasks even before* SHE *starts* HER *day.*

OLIMPIA: *(In a mumble)* As soon as I finish this. You can't just ask me to do what you want me to do, and interrupt what I'm doing. I don't stop from the time I wake up in the morning to the time I go

43

to sleep. You can't interrupt me whenever you want, not if you want me to get to the end of my work. I wake up at 5:30. I wash. I put on my clothes and make my bed. I go to the kitchen. I get the milk and the bread from outside and I put them on the counter. I open the icebox. I put one bottle in and take the butter out. I leave the other bottle on the counter. I shut the refrigerator door. I take the pan that I use for water and put water in it. I know how much. I put the pan on the stove, light the stove, cover it. I take the top off the milk and pour it in the milk pan except for a little. *(Indicating with* HER *finger)* Like this. For the cat. I put the pan on the stove, light the stove. I put coffee in the thing. I know how much. I light the oven and put bread in it. I come here, get the tablecloth and lay it on the table. I shout "Breakfast." I get the napkins. I take the cups, the saucers, and the silver out and set the table. I go to the kitchen. I put the tray on the counter, put the butter on the tray. The water and the milk are getting hot. I pick up the cat's dish. I wash it. I pour the milk left in the bottle in the milk dish. I put in on the floor for the cat. I shout "Breakfast." The water boils. I pour it in the thing. When the milk boils I turn off the gas and cover the milk, I get the bread from the oven. I slice it down the middle and butter it. Then I cut it in pieces *(indicating)* this big. I set a piece aside for me. I put the rest of the bread in the bread dish and shout "Breakfast." I pour the coffee in the coffee pot and the milk in the milk pitcher, except I leave *(indicating)* this much for me. I put them on the tray and bring them here. If you're not in the diningroom I call again. "Breakfast." I go to the kitchen, I fill the milk pan with water and let it soak. I pour my coffee, sit at the counter and eat my breakfast. I go upstairs to make your bed and clean your bathroom. I come down here to meet you and figure out what you want for lunch and dinner. And try to get you to think quickly so I can run to the market and get it bought before all the fresh stuff is bought up. Then, I start the day.

CRIMES OF THE HEART   Beth Henley

Fall, five years after Hurricane Camille. The kitchen in the MaGrath sisters' house in smalltown Hazlehurst, Mississippi. BABE BOTRELLE *(24), anxious and hysterical, tells* HER *older sisters about a suicide attempt that turned into the attempted murder of* HER *husband* ZACKERY.

BABE: And we were just standing around on the back porch playing with Dog. Well, suddenly Zackery comes from around the side of the house. And he startled me 'cause he's supposed to be away at the office, and there he is coming from round the side of the house. Anyway, he says to Willie Jay, "Hey, boy, what are you doing back here?" And I say, "He's not doing anything. You just go on home, Willie Jay! You just run right on home." Well, before he can move, Zackery comes up and knocks him one right across the face and then shoves him down the porch steps, causing him to skin up his elbow real bad on that hard concrete. Then he says, "Don't you ever come around here again, or I'll have them cut out your gizzard!" Well, Willie Jay starts crying—these tears come streaming down his face—then he gets up real quick and runs away, with Dog following off after him. After that, I don't remember much too clearly; let's see . . . I went on into the living room, and I went right up to the davenport and opened the drawer where we keep the burglar gun . . . I took it out. Then I—I brought it up to my ear. That's right. I put it right inside my ear. Why, I was gonna shoot off my own head! That's what I was gonna do. Then I heard the back door slamming and suddenly, for some reason, I thought about Mama . . . how she'd hung herself. And here I was about ready to shoot myself. Then I realized—that's right, I realized how I didn't want to kill myself! And she—she probably didn't want to kill herself. She wanted to kill him, and I wanted to kill him, too. I wanted to kill Zackery, not myself. 'Cause I—I wanted to live! So I waited for him to come on into the living room.

Then I held out the gun, and I pulled the trigger, aiming for his heart but getting him in the stomach. *(After a pause)* It's funny that I really did that.

DANNY AND THE DEEP BLUE SEA
John Patrick Shanley

The present. A bar in the Bronx. "The play is emotionally real but does not take place in a realistic world." ROBERTA *(31) wears blue jeans and a cheap dress-up blouse that's become ratty.* SHE *and* DANNY *have met at the bar and spent the night together.* BOTH *yearn for someone to speak to about the past and about the mistakes. Here* ROBERTA *tells* DANNY *about discovering a whale in the ocean. The story is a break from the violence that consumes* HER *life.*

ROBERTA: The ocean's right out there. *(A distant horn sounds)* See? That's a big boat goin' down some river to the ocean. That's what it is. There's boats right up by Westchester Square. What's that, twenty blocks? Look sometime, you'll see 'em. Not the real big ones, but big. Sea boats. I met a sailor in the bar one time. In the outfit, you know? I was all over him. But he turned out to be nothin—a pothead. He giggled a lot. It was too bad because ... Well, it was too bad. When we got married, me and Billy, that was my husband, we smoked a ball of opium one night. It really knocked me out. I fell asleep like immediately. And I dreamed about the ocean. It was real blue. And there was the sun, and it was real yellow. And I was out there, right in the middle of the ocean, and I heard this noise. I turned around, and whaddaya think I saw? Just about right next to me. A whale! A whale came shootin straight outta the water! A whale! Yeah! And he opened up his mouth and closed it while he was up there in the air. And people on the boat said, Look! The whales are jumpin! And no shit, these whales start jumpin outta the water all over the place. And I can see them! Through one a those round windows. Or right out in the open. Whales! Gushin outta the water, and the water gushin outta their heads, you know, spoutin! And then, after a while, they all stopped jumpin. It got quiet. Everybody went away. The water smoothed out. But I kept looking at the ocean. So deep and blue. And different. It was different then. 'Cause I knew it had all them whales in it.

THE DAY THEY SHOT JOHN LENNON
James McLure

Across the street from the Dakota apartment building in New York City. A light mist is falling. SALLY *(16) a white middle-class kid describes what* SHE *was doing when* SHE *heard the news that John Lennon had been murdered.* HER *heart is breaking for the first time.*

SALLY: I was doing my homework. I had a lot that night. I had a lot of geometry, I remember, and that's not my best subject anyway. I mean, I'm terrible at it if you want to know the truth. And I heard it on my T.V. you know? I had it down real low, 'cause my mom doesn't like me to play it when I'm doing my homework 'cause she says I can't concentrate. But I can. T.V. relaxes me. And then I heard the news vaguely in the background. And it didn't seem real. Maybe because it was T.V. I mean it was *realistic,* y'know, but it didn't seem *real.* I wanted to talk to Kevin, to talk to Kevin, to talk to someone to make it seem real. Kevin's my boyfriend. I mean, he used to be but then we broke up. It's a *long* story. Anyway I wanted to call Kevin and talk to him to express something, to make it *real,* because I had to make sense out of it, and I knew Kevin would understand. Kevin's very intense. Anyway my mother told me it was too late and I couldn't call him, and so I had to go to bed. *(Pause.)*

47

DEMIGOD   Richard LaGravenese

This monologue is from the musical A ... MY NAME IS
ALICE. *A* WOMAN *(20s-30s) speaks of* HER *ex-lover who is
leaving* HER *for another woman.* SHE *is so obsessed with him that*
SHE *thinks* SHE *sees him in the wash.*

WOMAN: I know you're gonna go .... I know it. I've been
thinking a lot about what you said and I believe that you love me too
.... And I understand that she gives you something else,
something you need I guess is what you said. I wanted to apologize
for yesterday. I was so confused, you know. I didn't know what
to do with myself ... I mean, two years ... what does a
person do? Do I have a nervous breakdown? Do I start a new career? Do I go and have an affair with O.J. Simpson? I mean what
do I do? I felt so ugly, Frank, and I don't mean just looks, I mean
ugly ... you know? Then you held me and touched the back of
my neck and kissed me and said the things you said, and I felt a lot
better. So, I did our laundry, like I always do on Sundays. And in
the middle of folding our bedspread, I noticed your jock strap in the
washing machine. Drowning in the wash cycle. It was twisting and
turning, being mangled and manipulated into all sorts of painful po-
sitions. It looked as if it were crying out for help, poor little thing.
Then the strangest thing ... I imagined you were still in it ...
the jock strap I mean. I got hysterical. I mean I couldn't stop
laughing. I thought it was the funniest thing I ever thought of.
... People started staring at me.... A woman came up to me
and said I should be careful not to inhale too much of that fabric
softener .... Then all of a sudden I heard your voice. So I ran
over to the machine, lifted the lid, and I could hear you in there,
choking on the Clorox 2 and the Lemon Fab. But I couldn't make
out what you were saying, so I yelled, "Frank, what is it, what are
you saying?" And the manager of the laundromat yelled back, "I'm
gonna call the police if you don't stop screamin' at your wash,

lady!" It made me think, Frank. It made me think that maybe I'm not handling this too well. I can't drop two years of being lovers and go back to being friends. We never were friends, Frank. We slept together on the first date, remember? And I know you wanted to leave on good terms, like telling me you still love me and all, but I really think it'll be easier for me if we break up as enemies. It'll be better for me just to hate you openly instead of being so adult about it, don't you think? I mean, why be adult about all this? So you can tell me about your lover and I can tell you about my lovers? So we can sleep together for old times' sake? I don't want to be your friend, Frank. I loved you, but I never said I liked you. And if being adult means throwing *me* away for that slut-rag you picked up on the goddamned train platform, then the most mature thing I could do for you would be to rip your face off. *(She mimes doing so)* Oh, yes! That feels much better!

DUET FOR ONE   Tom Kempinski

The present. The consulting room of DR. FELDMANN, *a psychiatrist.* STEPHANIE *(30s-40s), suffering from multiple sclerosis and confined to a wheelchair, has had* HER *career as a professional violinist cut short by the disease. Now there is a problem in* HER *marriage with the composer* DAVID LIEBERMANN. *Angry and bitter,* STEPHANIE *turns* HER *rage into a confrontation with* DR. FELDMANN.

STEPHANIE: Dr. . . . *(SHE clears her throat)* Dr. . . . *(SHE clears her throat)* What—er—what. I'm not clear . . . *(Suddenly SHE explodes)* JESUS CHRIST! What is this! What the hell is going on here, what are you bloody after anyway? I come here in good faith, I come because there may be a problem, I come willingly, openly . . . Do you have many patients at all, Dr. Feldmann, eh? Do you? Have you? I mean, *do* you, because as far

49

as I can see, you must be sending people out of here to see other doctors as fast as their legs, or their wheelchairs can carry them. I think you must send them to other doctors with a whole *new* set of illnesses and problems which you have specially and skillfully created by sheer determined hard work and bloody bloody-mindedness and insensitivity and rudeness, which I wouldn't have thought, though I am, of course not the great white-coated expert on the subconscious that you obviously mistakenly think you are, I would have thought . . . I mean I *wouldn't* have thought that those were the best attributes for helping people who are suffering, and don't think you've cleverly made me confess that I'm suffering, because *I'm not, repeat I'm not: not, savvy!* I mean is this some deeply clever, significant way way of trying to break up my marriage, is that your recipe for my condition, is that it, have I caught on? Or have you some potty theory you're testing out on me that by upsetting me . . . What . . . I have tried to tell you, I have *told* you . . . I mean, I . . . (SHE *stops abruptly with her* HER *mouth open, because* HER *mind has gone blank.* SHE *is stuck there for a moment, but the anger brings* HER *line of thinking back to mind)* Yes. Look! David, that's my husband David, you know, David Liebermann, you know, the world-famous composer, that Liebermann, right? He has a wonderful career right? In fact a brilliant, gleaming career, in fact, because, if I may say this in the presence of another one, he is a genius. He is undoubtedly one of the greatest composers of his age.

EXTREMITIES   William Mastrosimone

The present. The living room of an old-fashioned farmhouse set "Between Trenton and Princeton, New Jersey, where the cornfield meets the highway." MARJORIE (20s-30s) has fended off a brutal male rapist and has managed to capture and torture him. When HER

MARJORIE: Police. Charges. Arraignment. Lawyers. Money. Time. Judge. Jury. Proof. His word against mine. Defendant's attorney—a three-piece button down summa cum laude fresh from Harvard fuck-off: Did my client rape you? No. Assault you? Yes. How? With a pillow. Did you resist? Yes. Evidence? None. Witnesses? None. Did you tie him up? beat him? lock him in a fireplace? Six months for me, that animal goes free. And if I survive being locked up, then what do I do? Come home and lock myself up. Chainlock, boltlock, deadlock. And wait for him. Hear him in every creak of wood, every mouse in the wall, every twig tapping on the window. Start from sleep, 4 A.M. see something in the dark at the foot of my bed. Eyes black holes. Skin speckled gray like a slug. Hit the lights. He's not there. This time. So then what do I do? Wait for him? Or move three thousand miles, change my name, unlist my phone, get a dog. I don't want to taste my vomit everytime the doorbell rings. I don't want to flinch when a man touches me. I won't wear a goddam whistle. I want to live my life. He's never leaving this house.

FENCES   **August Wilson**

Pittsburgh 1957. ROSE *(40s), a black housewife, has just learned that* HER *husband of eighteen years,* TROY MAXSON, *has been seeing and sleeping with another woman.* ROSE *reacts to* TROY's *double standard and selfishness, offering* HER *own loyalty, fidelity and honesty as* HER *defense.*

[TROY: Rose, you're not listening to me. I'm trying the best I can to explain it to you. It's not easy for me to admit that I been standing in the same place for eighteen years.]

ROSE: I been standing with you! I been right here with you, Troy. I got a life too. I gave eighteen years of my life to stand in the same spot with you. Don't you think I ever wanted other things? Don't you think I had dreams and hopes? What about my life? What about me? Don't you think it ever crossed my mind to want to know other men? That I wanted to lay up somewhere and forget about my responsibilities? That I wanted someone to make me laugh so I could feel good? You not the only one who's got wants and needs. But I held on to you, Troy. I took all my feelings, my wants and needs, my dreams, and I buried them inside you. I planted a seed and watched and prayed over it. I planted myself inside you and waited to bloom. And it didn't take me no eighteen years to find out the soil was hard and rocky and it wasn't never gonna bloom. But I held on to you, Troy. I held you tighter. You was my husband. I owed you everything I had. Every part of me I could find to give you. And upstairs in that room with the darkness falling in on me, I gave everything I had to try and erase the doubt that you wasn't the finest man in the world. And wherever you was going I wanted to be there with you. 'Cause you was my husband, 'cause that's the only way I was gonna survive as your wife. You always talking about what you give and what you don't have to give. But you take too. You take and don't even know nobody's giving!

FOB   David Henry Hwang

The present. The back room of a Chinese restaurant in California. GRACE (19/20), a Chinese-American journalism student at UCLA, speaks of how SHE has come to terms with HER ethnic background and the prejudices SHE encountered.

GRACE: Yeah. It's tough trying to live in Chinatown. But it's tough trying to live in Torrance, too. It's true. I don't like being alone. You know, when Mom could finally bring me to the US, I was already ten. But I never studied my English very hard in Taiwan, so I got moved back to the second grade. There were a few Chinese girls in the fourth grade, but they were American-born, so they wouldn't even talk to me. They'd just stay with themselves and compare how much clothes they all had, and make fun of the way we all talked. I figured I had a better chance of getting in with the white kids than with them, so in junior high I started bleaching my hair and hanging out at the beach—you know, Chinese hair looks pretty lousy when you bleach it. After a while, I knew what beach was gonna be good on any given day, and I could tell who was coming just by his van. But the American-born Chinese, it didn't matter to them. They just giggled and went to their own dances. Until my senior year in high school—that's how long it took for me to get over this whole thing. One night I took Dad's car and drove on Hollywood Boulevard, all the way from downtown to Beverly Hills, then back on Sunset. I was looking and listening—all the time with the window down, just so I'd feel like I was part of the city. And that Friday, it was—I guess—I said, "I'm lonely. And I don't like it. I don't like being alone." And that was all. As soon as I said it, I felt all of the breeze—it was really cool on my face—and I heard all of the radio—and the music sounded really good, you know? So I drove home.

FOOL FOR LOVE   Sam Shepard

The present. A stark, low-rent motel room on the edge of the Mojave Desert, California. MAY (early-30s) and EDDIE are in love. But they share the same father. They have come to this motel room to fight out their love and hate. In the midst of battle between them, MAY stops to tell this story about THE OLD MAN, who is onstage but cannot be seen by MAY.

MAY: See, my mother—the pretty red-haired woman in the little white house with the red awning—was desperately in love with the old man. Wasn't she, Eddie? You could tell that right away. You could see it in her eyes. She was obsessed with him to the point where she couldn't stand being without him for even a second. She kept hunting for him from town to town. Following little clues that he left behind, like a postcard maybe, or a motel on the back of a matchbook. *(To* MARTIN*)* He never left her a phone number or an address or anything as simple as that because my mother was his secret, see. She hounded him for years and he kept trying to keep her at a distance because the closer these two separate lives drew together, these two separate women, these two separate kids, the more nervous he got. The more filled with terror that the two lives would find out about each other and devour him whole. That his secret would take him by the throat. But finally she caught up with him. Just by a process of elimination she dogged him down. I remember the day we discovered the town. She was on fire. "This is it!" she kept saying; "this is the place!" Her whole body was trembling as we walked through the streets, looking for the house where he lived. She kept squeezing my hand to the point where I thought she'd crush the bones in my fingers. She was terrified she'd come across him by accident on the street because she knew she was trespassing. She knew she was crossing the forbidden zone but she couldn't help herself. We walked all day through that stupid hick town. All day long. We went through every neighborhood, peering through every open window, looking in at every dumb family, until finally we found him.

(Rest)

It was just exactly suppertime and they were all sitting down at the table and they were having fried chicken. That's how close we were to the window. We could see what they were eating. We could hear their voices but we couldn't make out what they were saying. Eddie and his mother were talking but the old man never said a word. Did he, Eddie? Just sat there eating his chicken in silence.

[THE OLD MAN: *(To* EDDIE*)* Boy, is she ever off the wall with this one. You gotta' do somethin' about this.]

MAY: The funny thing was, that almost as soon as we'd found him—he disappeared. She was only with him about two weeks before he just vanished. Nobody saw him after that. Ever. And my mother—just turned herself inside out. I never could understand that. I kept watching her grieve, as though somebody'd died. She'd pull herself up into a ball and just stare at the floor. And I couldn't understand that because I was feeling the exact opposite feeling. I was in love, see. I'd come home after school, after being with Eddie, and I was filled with this joy and there she'd be—standing in the middle of the kitchen staring at the sink. Her eyes looked like a funeral. And I didn't know what to say. I didn't even feel sorry for her. All I could think of was him.

[THE OLD MAN: *(To* EDDIE*)* She's gettin' way outa' line, here.]

MAY: And all he could think of was me. Isn't that right, Eddie. We couldn't take a breath without thinking of each other. We couldn't eat if we weren't together. We couldn't sleep. We got sick at night when we were apart. Violently sick. And my mother even took me to see a doctor. And Eddie's mother took him to see the same doctor but the doctor had no idea what was wrong with us. He thought it was the flu or something. And Eddie's mother had no idea what was wrong with him. But my mother—my mother knew exactly what was wrong. She knew it clear down to her bones. She recognized every symptom. And she begged me not to see him but I wouldn't listen. Then she went to Eddie's mother and begged her. And Eddie's mother—*(Pause.* SHE *looks straight at* EDDIE*)*—Eddie's mother blew her brains out. Didn't she, Eddie? Blew her brains right out.

A GIRL'S GUIDE TO CHAOS   Cynthia Heimel

The present. New York City. CYNTHIA *(30), young, white, educated, single, post-feminist, and heterosexual, talks about the "fear of dating" in a monologue of the same title.*

CYNTHIA: The realization hits me heavily, like a .44 magnum smashing into my skull. My heart starts beating with a quick dread and my blood freezes in my veins. My stomach does backflips. I keep racing to the bathroom. The ordeal I am about to face is one of the most grisly, macabre and chilling experiences known to woman.

Dating. I will have to start dating again.

Please God no, don't make me do it! I'll be good from now on, I promise! I'll stop feeding the dog hashish! I'll be kind, thoughtful, sober, industrious, anything. But please God, not the ultimate torture of dating!

That's why I stayed with him so long, probably. I couldn't stand going through it all again. Sure, he might be a trifle wild and intractable, I kept telling myself, but at least I know I'll get laid tonight, and tomorrow night. At least someone will go to the movies with me and not try to hold my hand.

Hand-holding. The WORST thing about dating. The fellow, or maybe even I, will decide that holding hands is a sweet, simple way to start. Hah! It's the most nerve-wracking experience of life! Once I start holding hands, I'm afraid to stop. If I pull my hand away, will he think I'm being cold, or moody? Should I squeeze his hand and kind of wiggle my fingers around suggestively? Or is that too forward? What if we're holding hands in the movies and I have to scratch my nose? If I let his hand go, then scratch the offending nose, and then not grab his hand again immediately will he think I'm rejecting him? Will he be relieved? What if my hand is clammy? A clammy hand is more offensive than bad breath or right-wing politics. A clammy hand means you are a lousy lay! Everybody knows that!

And what, dear spiteful God, will I wear? I'll need new dresses, new jewelry, new sweaters, trousers, underwear. And shoes! Shoes tell everything, shoes have to be perfect! Men like high heels, right? I can't walk in high heels. Well, I can try. For a really important date, I can just see myself spending $250 on a pair of drop dead heels. This time will be different, I'll tell myself, this time I will be able to walk. But after an hour the ball of my foot will cramp up, I know it, and I'll hobble. "Is anything wrong?" he'll ask me solicitously, "you're limping." And I won't know where to look. I won't be able to say, "These fucking shoes are crippling me and if I don't take them off this minute I'll be maimed for life!" because then he'll know I just bought them, that I bought them to go out on a date with him. And that will make him feel weird and pressured to know that this date was a big deal for me and he'll realize that I'm not as popular and sophisticated as he thought I was if I had to buy a special pair of shoes that I can't even walk in for chrissakes just for a date with *him*. So I have to explain the limping in such a way that it won't have to do with shoes. An old war wound?

What if my hair refuses to behave? What if it's all recalcitrant and cranky and goes all limp and flat on one side and then sort of bends at a right angle over one ear? I mean, sometimes I apply precisely the right amount of mousse and hang upside down when I blow-dry it and yet something still goes drastically wrong and I end up looking like Margaret Thatcher. Sometimes the suspense of what I will look like is so terrible that I have to take a Valium.

I have been known to apply four shades of lipstick, one on top of the other, in a pathetic attempt to achieve a certain I'm-not-actually-wearing-lipstick-I-just-naturally-have-pink-moist-luscious-lips effect. I have been known to put green eye pencil below my lower lashes, look in the mirror, realize that I look like a gangrenous raccoon, quickly remove it, look in the mirror, realize that I'd rather look like a gangrenous raccoon than an anemic buffalo, and reapply the stuff.

I have been known to start trying on outfits in an entirely tidy room and somehow when I am finished every single item of clothing I own is off the rack and on the floor and then when the phone rings there is no way on earth I can find it. I can't even find my *bed*. God, I hate dating.

And when he rings my doorbell and my stockings are still around my ankles because my garter belt is missing but with mad, deep quick thought I finally remember it's in my black satin purse (don't ask) and I get it on and get the stockings up and answer the door smiling casually, what precisely do I say?

WHAT WILL I TALK ABOUT ON A DATE?

Not one thing that's on my mind will be a suitable topic of conversation. "Do you think we'll sleep together tonight?" "Are you one of those guys who can't make a commitment? Or can make a commitment to a woman with really smooth, finely muscled thighs?" "Is my deodorant working?" "What kind of relationship did you have with your mother?" "How do you think we're getting along so far?" "Do you like me?" "How much do you like me?" "Are you sure you really like me?" "Been exposed to any social diseases? Any problems with impotence?" "You're not going out with me because you feel sorry for me, are you?"

No, we'll talk about movies. What we've seen recently. What if he tells me that he finally got around to seeing *Cocoon* and it turned out to be one of the greatest experiences of his life? Will I pretend to agree? I bet I will. I bet something slimy inside myself will cause me to nod my head encouragingly and say "Yes, wasn't it lovely?" And then I'll hate myself because I've turned our date into a tissue of lies. I'll become distracted thinking about what a hypocrite I really am and my eyes will glaze over and I'll nod absently when he tries to draw me out and then he'll get all paranoid, thinking I hate him because he liked *Cocoon*. He'll be right.

But what if it turns out that his favorite movie is *The Man Who Came to Dinner*, with *Slapshot* a close second? Then I could fall in love. Then I'll really be terrified.

58

GHOST ON FIRE   Michael Weller

MICHELLE-MARIE *(mid-20s) is from Texas.* SHE *met her husband,* NEIL, *on the express line of a Taco Bell. They had an express marriage and express children. Three kids in five years.* HER *vacant life is gradually surrendering to drugs.*

MICHELLE: *(SHE talks to us, smoking a joint)* When you do a lot of driving like I do . . . see, where we live everything is pretty far away from everything else . . . *(tokes)* . . . like your house is here . . . and the mall is over there . . . school is over here, Timmy starts first grade next year, he's my firstborn, real real smart . . . *(tokes)* . . . oh, and tennis is like way across the valley, so when you ride the freeways a lot of hours every day you start to realize how much of your life you should spend being not really *at* somewhere but between somewhere and somewhere else, these pills, phew . . . *(tokes)* . . . one every four hours the guy said, one did nothing for this girl, it's three at a time or forget it, see, even at the very best of times I'm not what you'd call heavily into reality, Father Bonelli says it's not a good thing to run away from life and O.K. maybe he's got a valid point but on the other hand what the heck does a priest know about life . . . *(tokes)* . . . oh and this woman she lives next door and wears these like peasant blouses, Heidi in Sun City, it is too entirely bizarre . . . we have a great house . . . I think she makes pottery, yeah, that would explain the blouse, but her husband, what an unbelievable asshole always grabbing my tush and going "honk-honk, quality control, you pass" you know the type . . . but he's our neighbor so what are you gonna do . . . calls my husband "Ace", "Hey, Ace, I sure love to grab your wife's ass," I mean you don't go 'round doing things like that when you're a grown up . . . I am a mother of three, I am a grown up for pity's sake . . . *(tokes)* . . . The thing about reality like how I was saying . . . sometimes it can be very very painful, and who needs more pain; so it's Pill-Town for me, and Smokeville, and Powder-City . . . The Big Rock Candy Mountain. My mama used to sing that. *(beat)* Mama. *(beat)* Without a little help your heart could burst with the pain . . . *(tokes)* . . . and then like I'll just pull up to the place where I was driving to and presto, like magic, suddenly there I am: Somewhere! You know what I'm saying?

THE GRACE OF MARY TRAVERSE
Timberlake Wertenbaker

18th-Century·London. A drawing room of a prosperous City merchant. MARY (18) has been rigorously protected, groomed and educated by HER stern father. Alone, SHE walks back and forth across the carpet, trying to live up to his standards and perfect HER physical grace.

MARY: Almost.
  (SHE walks. Stops and examines)
Yes. Better.
  (SHE walks again. Looks)
Ah. There.
  (SHE walks faster now, then examines)
I've done it: see the invisible passage of an amiable woman.
  (Pause)
It was the dolls who gave me my first lessons. No well-made doll, silk-limbed, stain-clothed, leaves an imprint. As a child I lay still and believed their weightlessness mine. Awkward later to discover I grew, weighed. Best not to move very much. But nature was implacable. More flesh, more weight. Embarrassment all around. So the teachers came. Air, they said. Air? Air. I waited, a curious child, delighted by the prospect of knowledge. Air. You must become like air. Weightless. Still. Invisible. Learn to drop a fan and wait. When that is perfected, you may move, slightly, from

the waist only. Later, dare to walk, but leave no trace. Now my presence will be as pleasing as my step, leaving no memory. I am complete: unruffled landscape. I may sometimes be a little bored, but my manners are excellent. And if I think too much, my feet at least no longer betray this.

(SHE walks)

What comes after, what is even more graceful than air?

(SHE tries to tiptoe, then stamps the ground and throws her fan down) Oh damn!

HAWKER   Eric Overmyer

The present. A New York City street corner. LUCILLE (age unknown) a Hawker of Marvelous Inventions, appears before the audience dressed extravagantly. HER monologue is "A Four-minute Hector for One Woman".

LUCILLE: *(Formally)* Lucille? Is that you? *(Beat)* I just love pop music allusions, don't you? What have we here? *(She unpacks her wares. A glass.)*

LUCILLE: Oh, this is lovely. Cheese drink. It's to die. Sip? Cheddar shake. A little on the viscous side, I admit. Brie too is an acquired taste Whenever I'm in a room with a ripe brie I am reminded of an old boyfriend. But that is another story.

(SHE displays a medallion.)

LUCILLE: Thinking about Genghis puts me in mind of this. I know you're all going to want one. Yes, it's what you've all been waiting for, you've heard about it at the health club juice bar, wiping the carrot froth off your upper lip, you've read the subway ads in Spanish, you've wished for one at Area in the wee wee hours. Say no more. A detector of sexually transmitted diseases. Great. Am I right or what? Who needs the guess work? Life's too short. Changes colors just like those mood rings I sold you last time I was

61

here. Take it into Carumba's, it's Fourth of July fireworks. You have not seen colors like this since mescaline. I don't care what they say now, the sixties were not half bad. Let's see, what else?

(SHE displays a business card.)

LUCILLE: This is more in the line of a service rather than a good. It's an agent for your life. Somebody to negotiate for you at the cleaners, stand in line at the bureau of motor vehicles, the post office, the bank, Balducci's. Somebody to duke it out with your ex-, your present significant other, your boss, even with Mom.

Why do you have to be a rich and famous asshole to have your own personal major-domo? Is ten percent too much to pay for a stress-free environment? I think not!

(SHE puts card away.)

LUCILLE: *(High Dudgeon)* "Las cucarachas entran—Pero no pueden salir!"

(Beat)

I wish I knew the one for hemmorhoids. The last thing I need is hemmorhoids. Sounds so much better in Spanish, somehow.

(SHE puts on cardboard 3D glasses.)

LUCILLE: Nice, huh? At last they've found a use for those millions of glasses. These are for watching German art. They make it funny. They give it all those things German art inevitably lacks. Irony, a light touch, a spirit of fun—in short, a sense of humor. No longer is the phrase "German sense of humor" a horrible oxymoron thanks to these nifty little glasses. A must for Pina Bausch concerts or Kroetz plays. Just an aside—can you imagine having sex with either Pina Bausch or Franz Xaver Kroetz? They're at the top of my list to look out for.

(SHE straps on a red clown nose.)

LUCILLE: I know what you're thinking. Lucille—is that you? Oh, Lucille, come on. Please. A clown nose? We can get a clown nose at our favorite novelty emporium. What do we need with a clown nose? We depend on you, Lucille, for the scarce and unusual, the frightening and the purgative, the exquisitely absurd, the faintly ridiculous. Speaking of the exquisitely absurd, what are we all going to do now that Ronco has gone out of business? Vegamatic? The little gadget that scrambled the egg in the shell? Operators are standing by! Not available in any store! It really really works! *(Sighs)* An institution has passed. The end of an era. I hope all of you out there are holding on to your Vegamatics because they are WORTH SOMETHING NOW! Big buckage. Major league clammage. Boo-coo dinero.

(Shakes herself.)

Lucille, you sentimental old Bozo. You haven't even told the folks about the nose. And time is running out.

(SHE puts on a hat to go with her nose.)

LUCILLE: Feeling blue? Is "anomie" your middle name? Out of step and alienated? Hate the theatre? Wonder what planet the critics are from? Can't get it up to find *People* magazine a laff riot like you used to? Only mildly amused by *Enquirer* headlines like "Bo Derek—Herpes Scare!"? Find you're not surprised by the *Times* article that 50% of America does not believe in evolution? Feel trapped in New York, because bad as it is, you know at least three people who laugh at the same appalling shit you do? Wonder why no one seems to notice that our acting president isn't playing with a full deck? I know what ails you, Bunky. I know about that free-floating anxiety, that subtle sunset depression. I know it's not your relationship with your mother that's got you down—it's the state of the union.

(Taps her nose.)

You may think this is a clown nose—but it's not. It is an Irony Relaxer. And that seems to me to be a necessity for modern life. Wear it to the theatre, wear it to the laundromat, wear it while reading the *Times,* or better yet, the *Post,* wear it while watching TV news, wear it watching the Ron and Nancy Show, wear it watching Mary Lou Retton, wear it whenever you just cannot fucking believe it. You'll feel better. It really really works. Not available in any store. Operators are standing by.

(Beat)

Yes, I know one must have a sense of irony to survive. But sometimes you just got to give it a rest.

(SHE collects her stuff.)

LUCILLE: My four minutes are up. Gotta run.

(for Brenda Wehle)

HIGHEST STANDARD OF LIVING
Keith Reddin

The present. A small apartment in a Russian city. LUDMILLA (30s-40s), a Russian doctor, has invited an American student to dinner. During the evening SHE begins to get a bit drunk and starts to reveal HER paranoia about life in a police state.

LUDMILLA: I saw something today. At the bus stop. On the way to the hospital. There are maybe three or four people waiting with me. One man he keeps staring at the others and listening, and I think to myself he is watching everything a little too hard. He is so serious. And I think he is from the police, to listen what other people say. I think every day at bus stops are the police watching and listening and today at this bus stop it is this man. I look quick at the others waiting and they look at me, and I see in their eyes, in a tiny second of this look, that they know too. So we wait. Now we are getting very nervous. And we all think we must talk, so that we show we do not know that this secret policeman is watching us. But we must always only talk about innocent things, stupid things. An old man comes up to the bus stop. It is hot out, and he is sweating and trying to breathe and he smiles at us and he says "It is so oppressive I can't hardly breathe." We all look at each other. The policeman says to the old man "Yes it is, it is hard to breathe."

We hold our breath. The old man not knowing what is happening says, "Yes, so hard to breathe." And the agent grabs the old man very hard by the arm and starts to lead him away. And the old man and the agent disappear as they turn the corner. Because here there are certain words that cannot be spoken out loud. They take on bigger meaning. And everyone at the bus stop knows this and looks at their feet and are silent as the old man disappears, maybe forever. Then I began to fear that everyone at that bus stop was watching me. Watching to see my reaction to this scene. This incident was performed for my benefit and the agent leaves so that people can then hear me express my reaction to this arrest.

HUNTING COCKROACHES   Janusz Glowacki

The present. New York. A squalid, shabby apartment during the night. A map of America hangs on the wall. ANKA (30s-40s), a Polish émigré actress, is sitting on the bed looking quizzically at the audience. HER husband, JAN, is lying next to HER asleep. HER monologue opens the play.

ANKA: *(Recites from* MACBETH *and looks at* HER *hands)*: Yet here's a spot .... Out damned spot! Out, I say! One—two— why then 'tis time to do't! Hell is murky! Fie, my lord, fie! A soldier, and afeard! ... What, will these hands ne'er be clean? No more o' that, my lord, no more o' that; you mar all with this starting.... Here's the smell of the blood still: all the perfumes of Arabia will not sweeten this little hand. Oh! Oh! Oh! ... Wash your hands, put on your nightgown; look not so pale. I tell yet again, Banquo's buried; he cannot come out of the grave ... To bed, to bed; there's knocking at the gate. Come, come, come, come, give me your hand. What's done cannot be undone. To bed, to bed, to bed.
[JAN: Turn off the light.]

ANKA *(To audience)*: My name is Anka. I can't sleep. I'm a nervous wreck. I'm Polish. I've been in New York for three years. For the past three months I can't get any sleep. I mean, at first I couldn't sleep for something like a month, then I could, and then I couldn't and then I could again. Now for the past forty-two days—or maybe it's twenty-two days—I can't sleep at all. *(Studying the audience)* I'm an actress ... I can't get any parts due to my accent. They say I have an awful accent ... do I? That's my husband, Janek .... *(Points to him)* He can't sleep either. He's just pretending he's asleep .... *(Smiles)* I know it. He can't fall asleep without his pills and I hid them. *(Looks around, pulls a bottle of pills from under the mattress, and shows them to audience)* See! *(Smiles triumphantly)* To tell the truth the pills don't help him any, but he loves searching for them. He's a writer .... He was very famous in Poland ... a novel of his came out in Paris .... One of his plays was produced in New York,. *(Looks around the audience)* His name is Krupinski, Jan Krupinski. *(Pauses for a moment; spells it out)* K-R-U-P-I-N-S-K-I .... Never heard of him? It's a good thing he's asleep. I mean, he's pretending .... Look, I've got a whole bunch of reviews. He got a very good one in *The New York Times,* and a real bad one in *The Village Voice.* I got an award for my interpretation of Lady Macbeth in Warsaw. I know it's completely moronic but here in America you have to praise yourself, right? If you don't have any confidence in yourself, who's going to. Do I really have an awful accent? I did some work for an art critic from Poland who's well connected, he works in an Italian restaurant at Second Avenue and 88th Street. He got me a temporary job at the Museum of Immigration. I'd appear every noon dressed as a nineteenth-century Polish emigrant. *(Ironically)* You know the outfit ... babushka, boots. But now the museum is being repaired .... *(Throws up HER hands as if to say. "What can I do?")* Isn't he good at pretending he's asleep. I taught him how. If it gets out he can't sleep, we're finished. In New York everybody knows how to sleep. I'm trying to get him to pretend he's happy. In New York everybody's happy. *(Jan groans)* In the daytime he usually sits in front of the map. *(Points to the map hanging on the wall. SHE gets up and goes over to the map for a while in silence)* Then he says: "What a strange country!" That's all. "What a strange country!" I told him he'd never make it here because he doesn't have a sincere smile. Everybody here has a sincere smile. And he's got a nasty one. He took it very hard. In Eastern Europe nobody has a sincere smile, except drunks and informers. *(Smiles)* Yesterday he sat in front of the map and practiced the art of the sincere smile, checking it every so often in the mirror. I told him he should write a play about Polish émigrés, but he said the subject is boring, either you make it or you don't.

HURLYBURLY   David Rabe

The time is "a little while ago." The living room of a small house in the Hollywood Hills owned by EDDIE *and* MICKEY. DARLENE *(30), beautiful and fashionable, is a photo-journalist who has been sleeping with both men. In this first monologue,* DARLENE *is talking to* EDDIE *about* HER *abortion and* HER *confusion over whether or not it was the right thing to do. In the second monologue,* BONNIE *(30s), a woman who is the complete opposite to* DARLENE, *comes up to the house to get some drugs and ends up going out with* EDDIE's *recently separated friend,* PHIL. SHE *talks about what happened after the "date" with* PHIL *turned into a nightmare.* SHE *was thrown out of a moving car and was bruised and battered.*

DARLENE: I had a, you know—and that was—well, rough, so I have some sense of it, really, in a very funny way.
[EDDIE *(As he goes into his bedroom)*: What?]

67

DARLENE: My abortion. I got pregnant. I wasn't sure exactly which guy—I wasn't going crazy or anything with a different guy every night or anything, and I knew them both very well, but I was just not emotionally involved with either one of them, seriously. *(Emerging from the bedroom, he freezes, staring down at her, his shirt half off)* Though I liked them both. A lot. Which in a way made the whole thing even more confusing on a personal level, and you know, in terms of trying to figure out the morality of the whole thing, so I finally had this abortion completely on my own without telling anybody, not even my girlfriends. I kept thinking in my mind that it wasn't a complete baby, which it wasn't, not a fully developed person, but a fetus which it was, and that I would have what I would term a real child later, but nevertheless, I had these nightmares and totally unexpected feelings in which in my dreams I imagined the baby as this teenager, a handsome boy of real spiritual consequences, which now the world would have to do without, and he was always like a refugee, full of regret, like this treasure that had been lost in some uncalled-for way, like when a person of great potential is hit by a car. I felt I had no one to blame but myself, and I went sort of out of my mind for a while, so my parents sent me to Puerto Rico for a vacation, and I got myself back together there enough to come home with my head on my shoulders at least semi-straight. I was functional, anyway. Semi-functional, anyway. But then I told everybody what had happened. I went from telling nobody to everybody.

* * *

[EDDIE: You must have done SOMETHING.]
BONNIE: I SAT THERE. *(Behind the bar, SHE drinks, puts ice on HER wounds)* He drove; I just listened to the music on the tape deck like he wanted, and I tol' him the sky was pretty, just trying, you know, to put some sort of fucking humanity into the night, some sort of spirit so we might, you know, appear to one another as

having had at one time or another a thought in our heads and were not just these totally fuck-oriented, you know, things with clothes on.

[EDDIE: What are you getting at?]

BONNIE: What I'm getting at is I did nothing, and in addition, I am normally a person who allots a certain degree of my energy to being on the alert for creeps, Eddie. I am not so dumb as to be ignorant of the vast hordes of creeps running loose in California as if every creep with half his screws loose has slid here like the continent is tilted. But because this guy was on your recommendation, I am caught unawares and nearly maimed. That's what I'm getting at. I mean, this guy is driving, so I tell him we can go to my house. He says he's hungry, so I say, "Great, how about a Jack-In-The-Box?" He asks me if that's code for something. So I tell him, "No, it's California-talk, we have a million of 'em, is he new in town?" His answer is, do I have a water bed? "No," I tell him, but we could go to a sex motel, they got water beds. They got porn on the in-house video. Be great! So then I detect he's looking' at me, so I smile, and he says, "Whata you smilin' about?" I say, "Whata you mean?" He says, like he talkin' to the steering wheel, "Whata you thinkin'?" or some shit. I mean, but it's like to the steering wheel; he's all bent out of shape.[. . .] *(Hitting at him with* HER *pantyhose)* I smiled, Eddie, for chrissake, I smiled is what I did. It's a friendly thing in most instances, but for him it promotes all this paranoid shit he claims he can read in it my secret opinions of him, which he is now saying. The worst things anybody could think about anybody, but I ain't saying nothing. He's sayin' it. Then he screams he knew this venture was a one-man operation and the next thing I know he's trying to push me out of the car. He's trying to drive it, and slow it down, and push me out all at once, so we're swervin' all over the road. So that's what happened. You get it now?

IN PLACE   Corinne Jacker

The present. The living room of DAISY STODDARD's *boarding
house.* DAISY *(30s-40s) is preparing breakfast for* JERRY, *one of
HER boarders. He is working on a computer game.* DAISY *inter-
rupts him with* HER *talk about the romance of gambling.*

DAISY: You know how you get a feeling of romance—a sniff of
aftershave lotion does it for me—I have that feeling right now.
[JERRY: Not while I'm working, Daisy.]
DAISY: Somewhere in a casino downtown, right at this very
minute, there's a machine and it is saying come on, play me, come
on, the jackpot's ready to go. It's ten, maybe twenty quarters down
the line. And it's beckoning to me, saying come on, lover, come
on, get into a cab and come on down here, I'm waiting, all hot and
juicy. Come on lover. And I would, I'd run to my red-hot machine
and drop my lucky quarter and get my fingers around that handle
and just squeeze it down. The quarters would pour out, a silver
stream of them right into my handbag. Overflow it. I'm down on
the floor, scooping up all the treasure. The big win of the day. But
I can't go. Because I don't know which casino it is, just that it's
there. My lucky day. Days like this only come up once, maybe
twice in a lifetime. And I am standing at this formica-topped table
pouring orange juice for a blackjack nut and a soon-to-be-divorcee.

LADY DAY AT EMERSON'S BAR AND GRILL
Lanie Robertson

1959. Midnight. A small bar in South Philadelphia. BILLIE
HOLIDAY *(44), the black American blues singer, stands before a
piano. HER career is on the downslide. In between songs SHE
tells the audience about the past. This story involves what it was
like being a black singer with an all white band touring the South.*

BILLIE: Easy livin'. Like the times I was singin' with Artie's band. Artie Shaw. An' we toured, see. We started out in Boston an' it was all down hill from that. In Boston, see, I had to sit in the bus till it was time for my numbers 'cause they didn't want no black bitch sittin' up on the bandstand with all those fellahs in the band which was all-white, see, so you can imagine when we got down to Virginia, North an' South Carolina an' Georgia an' worse. Anyway, there was this fancy restaurant we went into outside of Birmingham an' Artie an' the boys just couldn't have been sweeter or squarer with me. Places where they wouldn't let me in the front door none of them'd use the front door neither. An' if I had to sit out in the kitchen to get some eats the whole bunch of them'd sit out there too. So that always pissed off the ofays who ran the places anyway, see. So this one place we went to we was all sittin' out in the kitchen with all the colored help runnin' around us tryin' to do their jobs in that place just like we wasn't there. An' it was hot as hell in that kitchen anyway, and of course none of this treatment was free you know. We was all payin' top price for this, just like we was sittin' out front with all the grays. Only we was in the kitchen because Artie Shaw had this black bitch called Billie Holiday in his troupe. So everything was smooth as silk till I realized all of a sudden I had to use the bathroom in the worst way. I mean, my kidneys was almost to bust an' float me outta there right into the main dining room an' I knew damn well they didn't want that. So I got up an' asked this black dude who looked like he might have had some sense where was the bathroom an' he asked me why I wanted to know, thereby provin' he didn't have any more sense than I had in askin'. I shoulda found it on my own. Anyway, while I was tryin' to explain to him that I didn't really need to go there to powder my nose, if that's what was worryin' him. That it was for a more essential reason than that, when this blond bitch comes in the kitchen from the dining room. Somebody musta heard me askin' this dude an' run off to get this bitch to bring her into the discussion. Now, she was the maitresse dee who wouldn't let us into the dining room to begin with. So she saunters up real big, still clutchin' all these big red plush covered menus under her left tit and says, "Just what exactly seems to be the trouble here?" An' I look at her, see, like where'd the fuck she come from an' go, "The trouble seems to be that this dude can't answer a simple question." So then I knew somebody had ran to get her 'cause she says, "I'm sorry, Miss Day, but we don't have toilets for the colored." An' I said, "Listen, honey, you have me confused. I'm not Doris Day. I'm Billie Holiday. Lots of folks has said she an' me resembles each other, but this is the first time I know of where anybody's talked to the one an' thought they was talkin' to the other. Also I don't want to cast no aspersions on anybody workin' here or hurt anybody's feelin's or nothin' but ever' body I see workin' here 'cept you is about as colored as they come. Now, where do they go?" So she gives me this sweet little smile out of one side of her mouth an' says, "Yes, but they're males. We don't have a toilet for colored females." I said, "Honey, at this point I don't care if it's nothin' but a urinal or a dark corner of the room. Lead me to it, please. I'm about to bust." So she shifts her weight around slow, see, in this real tight black sequin-covered dress she's wearin' with sequin high-heel shoes to match an' tells me, "We didn't want you comin' in our restaurant to start with. We don't allow colored here. We only let you in because Mr. Shaw agreed to pay twice as much for all of you if we'd let you eat out here in the kitchen. Otherwise you wouldn't even be here. Now, if Mr. Shaw wants to do that, that's his business. But he said nothing about letting you use the phone, or the bar, or the dining room or the men's toilet, and I'm not going to let you do that." So I said, "Listen, Mr. Shaw's been very sweet. He's done a lot of nice things like this for me, and I appreciate it. But one thing I know of he can't do for me and that's piss. So what do you propose I do about this situation?" An' she give me that sweet little twisted side of her mouth smile and clutched a firm grip on that stack of menus and said, "Why don't you sit on it!" I was so shocked. I just looked at her a minute and then I said, "No. I think I'll let you do that." An I cut loose the biggest deluge all acrossed those sequined shoes of hers to come down the pike since Noah. You never seen a grown woman leap so high up in the air as she did in your life. Droppin' menus and screechin' like she'd been scalded all over the legs and feet by molten lead. An' all the boys in the band was on their feet ajumpin' up and down and hooting an carryin' on like we just won the second coming of the Civil War an' that was I assure you the high an' low of the whole tour for me. After that everybody in the band started sayin' "Watch out for Billie. She's got a secret weapon. She'll spoil your shoes quicker'n you can pay to get 'em polished" an' all kinda silly shit like that. But I loved 'em. They was pals to this black bitch an' I'll never forget it.

LATER

Corinne Jacker

The present. A beach, Rhode Island. MOLLY *(60s) a former teacher, reflects on the recent death of* HER *husband* MALACHI. SHE *is alone, in need, and desperate. Before* SHE *speaks* SHE *gives a soft cry aloud.*

MOLLY: There's no privacy in that house. A person can be more alone out here, in the full light of the moon, than in the darkest room in there. What's a person to do? Malachi gone and I can't stop my thoughts. Or my—needing. I won't ever be alone. He's here. Still. When we'd buried him, I washed the walls, and the floors, scrubbed and waxed. And all the linens, but he's still all the way through everything. Malachi, Malachi . . . foolish name for a man this day and age. I can still smell him. It won't go away. I think, maybe, it's gotten to be part of me. I raise my hand, and I sniff at the flesh, and it's him! You think, if the things are gone, then the memories have to be. I threw out the sheet. The one that was on his bed when he died. Just as it was, soiled, stinking, I put it in a plastic bag, and then I put the plastic bag into another plastic bag, and then the whole mess into a thick green trash bag, and then into the garbage. Damn him! I have to come out here to sleep. Memories. Always the same, over and over. And I'm not safe, even here, by the sea. The cry in the night. And I didn't want to wake up. You drank too much again, I thought. All right, clean up your own mess this time. But then, he was sick. Really sick .... Why can't I bury this part, deep in the sand, out of me. Him being sick, and touching me again, so gently, as if he was really ashamed, and saying it wasn't the drink, it was something else, something funny, and wouldn't I hold his hand. I took his hand, but not easily. And I said, you'll never learn, will you, Mal? You should take the aspirin before you go to bed. And have a glass of milk before you start the drinking .... I should have known. He never asked me to take his hand like that, like a boy. *(From out on the beach, the sound of some boys, drunk on beer, singing "Roll Me Over, In the Clover.")* When it was good, it was a different kind of thing entirely .... The time he got out of the shower and strutted around with no towel, singing the *Liebestod* at the top of his lungs because the girls were at camp and I was the only one to hear it. And I came in with his hot toddy, and the whole bathroom was steamy, and the wet grew on my skin like mould. And he made me sing with him—I can't carry a tune or even make it through *Happy Birthday to You,* but I sang that duet. The steam fogged up my glasses. And when I took them off, there was his face, bigger than life, his mouth open, close enough to bite me. Back off, I said. My eyes are crossing. And he did, he nipped at my nose like a little puppy, and turned his back .... So slender, with a dark brown birthmark spotched over the left side, like a pool of bitter chocolate. Well, he's in the ground. I won't see it again.

A LESSON FROM ALOES   Athol Fugard

The present. Aloga Park, a lower middle class suburb of Port Elizabeth, South Africa. GLADYS (40s) has been recovering from a nervous breakdown. SHE records events in a diary as a means of therapy. HER husband, PIET, asks HER to read the events of the week. What GLADYS has recorded is a world of emptiness and boredom.

GLADYS: This hasn't been such a good week. Let's see . . . an old woman looking for work, the meter reader . . . who else? Oh yes! Those little black boys selling brooms and baskets. But they're always around. Last week I had a gentleman from the Watchtower Society at the front door. That was a long talk. I was a bit nervous at first because he asked if he could come in, but he turned out to be very nice. Do you know they've got a date worked out for the end of the world? It's not far off, either. I almost told him there are times when I think it has already happened. *(PIET smiles)* I'm not joking. It can be very quiet here in the house when you're at work. If I haven't got the radio on or a car isn't passing in the street, it's hard sometimes to believe there is a world out there full of other people. Just you and me. That's all that's left. The streets are empty and I imagine you wandering around looking for another survivor. If you ever find one, Peter, you must bring him home.

LES LIASONS DANGEREUSES
Christopher Hampton

18th-Century Paris. The salon of MME LA MARQUISE DE MERTEUIL. SHE is entertaining one of HER former lovers, VALMONT. MERTEUIL (30s) is beautiful, manipulative and extremely clever. A widow, here SHE reflects on how SHE has culti-

vated HER *sexual wiles as a way to dominate men.*

[VALMONT: I often wonder how you managed to invent yourself.]
MERTEUIL: I had no choice, did I, I'm a woman. Women are obliged to be far more skillful than men, because who ever wastes time cultivating inessential skills? You think you put as much ingenuity into winning us as we put into losing: well, it's debatable, I suppose, but from then on, you hold every ace in the pack. You can ruin us whenever the fancy takes you: all we can achieve by denouncing you is to enhance your prestige. We can't even get rid of you when we want to: we're compelled to unstitch, painstakingly, what you would just cut through. We either have to devise some way of making you want to leave us, so you'll feel too guilty to harm us; or find a reliable means of blackmail: otherwise you can destroy our reputation and our life with a few well-chosen words. So of course I had to invent: not only myself, but ways of escape no one else has ever thought of, not even I, because I had to be fast enough on my feet to know how to improvise. And I've succeeded, because I always knew I was born to dominate your sex and avenge my own.
[VALMONT: Yes; but what I asked you was how.]
MERTEUIL: When I came out into society I'd already realized that the role I was condemned to, namely to keep quiet and do as I was told, gave me the perfect opportunity to listen and pay attention: not to what people told me, which was naturally of no interest, but to whatever it was they were trying to hide. I practiced detachment. I learned how to smile pleasantly while, under the table, I stuck a fork into the back of my hand. I became not merely impenetrable, but a virtuoso of deceit. Needless to say, at that stage nobody told me anything: and it wasn't pleasure I was after, it was knowledge. But when, in the interests of furthering that knowledge, I told my confessor I'd done 'everything', his reaction was so appalled, I began to get a sense of how extreme pleasure might be. No sooner had I made this discovery than my mother announced my marriage:

so I was able to contain my curiosity and arrived in Monsieur de Merteuil's arms a virgin.

All in all, Merteuil gave me little cause for complaint: and the minute I began to find him something of a nuisance, he very tactfully died.

I used my year of mourning to complete my studies: I consulted the strictest moralists to learn how to appear; philosophers to find out what to think; and novelists to see what I could get away with. And finally I was well placed to perfect my techniques.

[VALMONT: Describe them.]

MERTEUIL: Only flirt with those you intend to refuse: then you acquire a reputation for invincibility, whilst slipping safely away with the lover of your choice. A poor choice is less dangerous than an obvious choice. Never write letters. Get them to write letters. Always be sure they think they're the only one. Win or die.

A LIE OF THE MIND　　　　　　　Sam Shepard

An isolated house somewhere in the American West. In the first monologue LORRAINE *(50s-60s) sits beside* HER *grown son* JAKE, *spoon-feeding him from a bowl of* HER *cream of broccoli soup.* JAKE *has returned home in a state of depression and confusion after trying to kill his wife,* BETH. *In the second monologue,* SALLY *(20s),* JAKE's *sister, comforts* HER *mother* LORRAINE *with the same bed-side soup.* SHE *tells* LORRAINE *about how* SHE *and* JAKE *went down to Mexico in search of their father.* SHE *has just gotten to the point of confronting their father in his trailer.*

LORRAINE: *(Holding spoon of soup at his mouth)* Here now, come on. Just try a sip. That's all I'm askin'. Just a simple sip. I'm not askin' for the whole bowl. We'll work up to that slow. Just a little tiny old sip for now. Jake? *(Harder)* Sit up here and drink this soup! I'm sick of babyin' you. This is your favorite. Cream of broccoli. I made it special in the blender.

(Pause. JAKE refuses soup)

I don't know why in the world you insist on gettin' so worked up over a woman. Look at you. I have never in my life seen you lookin' so let-down. You musta lost a good thirty, forty pounds. A woman ain't worth that kind of a loss. Believe you me. There's more pretty girls than one in this world. Not that she was such a looker. I can't even remember what she looked like to tell you the truth, but she couldn'ta been all that great. You'll find someone else sooner or later. You're a strong, strappin' man yet. Got a little age on you now but that don't matter when you got a strong frame. Your daddy was still lookin' good at the age of sixty, even though the bottle had walked across his face a few times over. His face was a mess, I'll admit that. I'll be the first to admit that. But he still had that big stout frame on him, just like you got. Still managed to twirl my ticket, I'll tell ya that much. Somebody's bound to come along, just dyin' to be encircled by them big bony arms. Don't you worry about that one bit. Now, come on, just try this soup. Just do me a little favor, all right? Do you want me to play helicopter with it like we used to?

(SHE raises the spoon of soup over his head and starts making helicopter sounds as JAKE watches the spoon from below.)

LORRAINE: *(In a pinched cartoon voice)* Man overboard! Man overboard! Looks like he could be drownin'! Better lower down the life-support. Take it slow, we don't wanna lose him now.

(JAKE suddenly knocks the spoon out of HER hand and sends it flying. He rips the blanket and sheet off himself, grabs the bowl out of HER hand, stands on the bed, holds the bowl high above his head and sends it crashing down on the mattress. Then he begins to stomp on the soup, jumping all over the bed, exhaling loudly and grunting like a buffalo. LORRAINE backs off fast and stands there watching him. JAKE finally expends all his energy and just stands

78

there limply on the bed, bent forward at the waist, arms dangling and gasping for air.)

LORRAINE: *(Away from him, keeping* HER *distance)* What in the name of Judas Priest is the matter with you, boy! I spent hours makin' that stuff. I slaved over the blender tryin' to get it creamy and smooth, just how you like it! Look what you've done to that soup!

* * *

SALLY: Maybe. Maybe *you* can. That's what Jake tried to do. He's a lot like you I guess. He started squirming in that trailer. Making up reasons why we had to get outa there. Get back across the border before it got dark. Dad kept wanting us to stay but he didn't have anything to offer us. And that's when Jake made a desperate move. He didn't even know he was doing it. He was so desperate to get out of that situation, that he stands up and he offers to take Dad and me out to a bar. For a drink! I couldn't believe it. Dad's whole face lit up. I've never seen his face like that. He smiled like a little kid and grabbed his hat.

[LORRAINE: You can't stop a drinkin' man from drinkin'. All he needs is an idea and he's gone. Just the idea of straddling a bar stool in some honky-tonk somewhere in his mind. He's gone.]

(LORRAINE slowly pulls herself up to a sitting position and listens more intently to SALLY.)

SALLY: They started right off with double shots of tequila and lime. At first it was like this brotherhood they'd just remembered. But then it started to shift. After about the fourth double shot it started to go in a whole different direction.

[LORRAINE: That figures.]

SALLY: There was a meanness that started to come outa both of them like these hidden snakes. A terrible meanness that was like—murder almost. It *was* murder.

[LORRAINE: Whad'ya mean, murder?]

SALLY: Their eyes changed. Something in their eyes. Like animals. Like the way an animal looks for the weakness in another animal. They started poking at each other's weakness. Stabbing. Just a little bit at a time. Like the way that rooster used to do. That rooster we had that went around looking for the tiniest speck of blood on a hen or a check and then he'd start pecking away at it. And the more he pecked at it the more excited he got until finally he just killed it.

[LORRAINE: Yeah, we had to boil that one. Tough son of a gun.]

SALLY: They locked into each other like there was nobody else in the bar. At first it was all about sports. About which one of them could throw a hardball faster. Which one could take the toughest hit in football. Which one could run the fastest and the longest. That was the one they decided would be the big test. They decided to prove it to each other once and for all. So they downed a couple more tequilas and crashed out through the doors of the place into the street. [. . .] Now it was like he'd had a transfusion or somethin'. That tequila went right into his blood and lit him on fire. He crouched down in a racing position right beside Jake. And they were both deadly serious. And they took off. Dad took about four strides and fell flat on his face in the street but Jake never stopped. He ran like a wild colt and never once looked back. Straight into the next bar up the block. I went over and tried to help Dad up but he turned on me and snarled. Just like a dog. Just exactly like a crazy dog. I saw it in his eyes. This deep, deep hate that came from somewhere far away. It was pure, black hate with no purpose. [. . .] He wouldn't let me help him. He just crawled up the street toward the bar that Jake went into. And there I was following along behind. I felt so stupid. He kept turning and snarling at me to keep back. But I didn't wanna fall too far back 'cause I was afraid somethin'—

(SHE *starts to break down but stops herself.*)

[LORRAINE: What?]

80

SALLY: *(Trying to control it)* I was afraid somethin' bad might happen to him and—it happened anyway.

[LORRAINE: What happened?]

SALLY: Jake came up with a brilliant idea. He said, since we were only about a mile from the American border we should hit every bar and continue the race until we got to the other side. First one to the other side, won. First one to America! But we couldn't miss a bar. Right then I knew what Jake had in mind.

[LORRAINE: What?]

SALLY: Jake had decided to kill him.

LITTLE VICTORIES   Lavonne Mueller

19th-century America. SUSAN B. ANTHONY, *one of the early advocates for women's votes, here talks of* HER *experiences travelling out West at a time when few women were there and life was one of extreme hardship.* SHE *survived and triumphed, but died in 1906 believing herself a failure. Women received the right to vote in 1920.* SHE *speaks in confidential tones.*

SUSAN B. ANTHONY: All the time. I'm lonely. I never thought I'd be lonely. *(Pause)* It seems like here in the West, you come upon a stranger . . . share his or her food and home . . . and you're no closer to that person than a bird and a squirrel who happen upon the same tree branch. *(Pause)*

There's always a kind of brakeman who's willing to slow down the switch engine for a few minutes so I can jump aboard a flatcar or gondola and hook a free ride to the next town. Sometimes I run for the caboose . . . huffing alongside, my cape flapping. I throw my bags at the platform and lunge at the handrails. *(Pause)* Too often the train glides away with my belongings. But my luggage is always left at the next depot up the line. *(Pause)*

I saw a cowboy mount his horse at the rack in front of my hotel, ride across the street to the Post Office, dismount and tie his horse, mail a letter, then mount again and ride the horse back across the street to the hotel, get off, tie the horse and go to his room. *(Pause)*

I had a long wait with a prairie farmer at the depot outside Comb Wash, and I gave him my whole speech. About the virtues of women. What our vote means to mankind, etcetera. A good sixty minutes worth. *(Pause)* When I finished . . . he said: "When I'm feeding the steers and drive the wagonload of hay there and find just one, I don't unload the whole thing for him." *(Pause)* A Westerner always speaks by way of his animals. *(Pause)*

I haven't earned a dollar in six days . . . I smell like a smoked side of bacon . . . I can grease a fry pan on my cape . . . I let a dog sleep on my feet to keep them warm. *(After a long pause)* I saw a bride today. She sat in a chair outside the church. And her husband knelt in front of her, and put his arms around her—chair and all. *(Pause)*

I dream . . . I never change anything. I see my face . . . old, weather-wrung. It's a homeless face. *(Pause)* I'm afraid . . . afraid to stop . . . afraid to go on. *(Pause)* A marshall's on my trail. *(Pause)* If he gets me, I'll be hobbled like a horse. Taken back East on the same overland coach I came on. People gawking at every stage station. Finally thrown in a dark cell in Rochester. Tried with the speed of a miner's court. *(Pause)* What if . . . I give up everything and lose? What if . . . I have no place to go . . . when I'm old.

LUNCH   Steven Berkoff

The present. A beach that could be anywhere. A MAN *and* WOMAN *enjoy a chance meeting. There is mutual attraction. But they are unable to relate on any other level apart from the physical. After a quick and torrid sexual encounter, the* WOMAN *berates the* MAN, *comparing him to* HER *own husband back home.*

WOMAN: You are a poisonous spider—you really are . . . poisonous. Yes, you even look like one—a crawling garden spider, no not garden—the thing that darts out of dirty cupboards, that you step on . . . FAST—yes you do . . . My husband loves me—yes he does—he loves me and soon it will be time to go home and prepare his supper—he comes keenly—lovingly in—expecting little kitchen noises and smells . . . he brings the cold wintry air in with him . . . smelling of train fumes and of Aqua de Selva—all fresh—a rough chin tickling me, his smells reassuring me—all familiar . . . and he loves me—really and hugely LOVES, and I make him his favorite meals his mother once made him and we eat and watch TV—not plays, or quiz shows, serious things, *Man Alive, Panorama*—we discuss them afterwards and he writes long eloquent letters to *The Times* about injustice—but they never publish them . . . He's full of goodness—exudes it like vapor—it clings to the walls of the room—every room . . . it reaches into the grain of the furniture—becomes part of them, part of me, so secure, cocoon-safe . . . six-ten each evening, his tinkling key in the lock, his hat on the stand faintly grease-stained—his himness coming in—hard, masculine himness wrapping the house with blankets of love . . . and just so he comes in the door, he whistles, so as not to alarm me, so I know it's him—not anyone else, but him—not a burglar or a murderer, a little whistle *(whistles three notes)* and if I'm in the kitchen I whistle back so he knows I'm there—not gone—not died—a victim of GBH or gang-bang angels leather-winged—but there in a perpetual way, like he faces me square on, direct and coming to me, always to me . . . even when not facing me he's coming to me, his thoughts, murmurs, hungers, desires, always reaching me and mine him, so our invisible webs are always gripped even miles apart . . . I finish his sentences, he collides with mine, anticipate his wants—I don't need anything else—don't certainly need you . . .

THE MARRIAGE OF BETTE AND BOO
Christopher Durang

Late at night. BETTE *(late 20s-30s) has been married to* BOO *for several years.* SHE *has just suffered* HER *second miscarriage and strains have appeared in their marriage. On an impulse and out of desperation,* BETTE *phones an old school friend,* BONNIE. SHE *tries to communicate with* BONNIE *over the distance of time and recapture some comforting moments from the past.*

BETTE: Hello, Bonnie? This is Betsy. Betsy. *(To remind her)* Bonnie, your grade is eight, and Betsy, your grade is five. Yes, it's me. How are you? Oh, I'm sorry, I woke you? Well, what time is it? Oh I'm sorry. But isn't Florida in a different time zone than we are? Oh. I thought it was. Oh well.

Bonnie, are you married? How many children do you have? Two. That's nice. Are you going to have any more? Oh, I think you should. Yes, I'm married. To Boo. I wrote you. Oh, I never wrote you? How many years since we've spoken? Since we were fifteen. Well, I'm not a very good correspondent. Oh, dear, you're yawning, I guess it's too late to have called. Bonnie, do you remember the beach and little Jimmy Winkler? I used to dress him up as a lamp shade, it was so cute. Oh. Well, do you remember when Miss Willis had me stand in the corner, and you stand in the wastebasket, and then your grandmother came to class that day? I thought you'd remember that. Oh, you want to go back to sleep?

Oh, I'm sorry. Bonnie, before you hang up, I've lost two babies. No, I don't mean misplaced, stupid, they died. I go through the whole nine month period of carrying them, and then when it's over, they just take them away. I don't even see the bodies. Hello? OH, I thought you weren't there. I'm sorry, I didn't realize it was so late. I thought Florida was Central Time or something. Yes, I got twelve in geography or something, you remember? Betsy, your grade is twelve and Bonnie, your grade is . . . what did you get in geography? Well, it's not important anyway. What? No, Boo's not home. Well, sometimes he just goes to a bar and then he doesn't come home until the bar closes, and some of them don't close at all and so he gets confused what time it is. Does your husband drink? Oh, that's good. What's his name? Scooter? Like bicycle? I like the name Scooter. I love cute things. Do you remember Jackie Cooper in *Skippy* and his best friend Sukey? I cried and cried. Hello, are you still there? I'm sorry, I guess I better let you get back to sleep. Goodbye, Bonnie, it was good to hear your voice. *(Hangs up. Lights change.)*

MA RAINEY'S BLACK BOTTOM
August Wilson

1927. A recording studio in Chicago. MA RAINEY *(40s), one of the all-time great blues singers, a heavy-set, proud, and domineering woman, tells of being used by her white manager.*

MA RAINEY: I been doing this a long time. Ever since I was a little girl. I don't care what nobody else do. That's what gets me so mad with Irvin. White folks try to be put out with you all the time. Too cheap to buy me a Coca-Cola. I lets them know it, though. Ma don't stand for no shit. Wanna take my voice and trap it in them fancy boxes with all them buttons and dials . . . and then too cheap to buy me a Coca-Cola. And it don't cost but a nickel a bottle.
[CUTLER: I knows what you mean about that.]
MA RAINEY: They don't care nothing about me. All they want is my voice. Well, I done learned that, and they gonna treat me like I want to be treated no matter how much it hurt them. They back there now calling me all kinds of names . . . calling me everything but a child of god. But they can't do nothing else. They ain't got what they wanted yet. As soon as they get my voice down on them

recording machines, then it's just like if I'd be some whore and they roll over and put their pants on. Ain't got no use for me then. I know what I'm talking about. You watch. Irvin right there with the rest of them. He don't care nothing about me either. He's been my manager for six years, always talking about sticking together, and the only time he had me in his house was to sing for some of his friends.

[CUTLER: I know how they do.]

MA RAINEY: If you colored and can make them some money, then you all right with them. Otherwise, you just a dog in the alley. I done made this company more money from my records than all the other recording artists they got put together. And they wanna balk about how much this session is costing them.

MY SISTER IN THIS HOUSE   Wendy Kesselman

1930s. Le Mans, France. LEA *(teens), wears a simple childlike dress and is working as a house maid in a middle class family.* SHE *writes a letter to* HER *sister,* CHRISTINE, *who is also in service and whom* SHE *misses very much.* SHE *describes the events in* HER *present life and* HER *desire to be with* CHRISTINE, *who is standing further away on stage.*

LEA: Dear Christine. When Maman left me here on Friday, I thought I would die. They didn't want to take me at first, but Maman told Madame Crespelle I was fifteen. Christine, I wish you could see what they eat. You can't imagine the desserts. The cook told me Madame's favorite dish is duck with cherries and Monsieur's, chicken with champagne. I'm hungry all the time. But it isn't as bad as I expected. I even have my own room. Do you think you could ask Madame Roussel to change your day off to Wednesday, like mine? *(SHE pauses)* Today Madame Crespelle smiled at me. She was pleased with how the silver looked. I had been polishing it all morning. It was worth every minute for Madame's smile. When she smiles she looks just like Sister Veronica. *(A bell rings)* Three days ago Maman came and took me away. She said I could earn more money somewhere else. I was just getting used to the Crespelles, but I'm getting four more francs a month and Maman's promised to let me keep one of them. The Cottins have one daughter, Mademoiselle Sophie. Her birthday is next week. She's only two months older than me. She's so pretty. Her skin is like milk. And Christine, you should hear her play the piano. *(SHE pauses)* Madame Cottin counts everything. Even the chocolates in the glass bowl. But I remember everything you taught me. And I think Madame will be pleased with me. *(SHE pauses)* Every morning Madame Cottin examines my fingernails before I make the beds. Her things are so delicate. So many ruffles. So many buttons. You wouldn't believe how many buttons. It takes me two hours to iron one dress. And even then Madame isn't satisfied. *(SHE pauses)* In this house I'm always afraid I'll do something wrong. Not like you, Christine. You never make mistakes. *(SHE pauses)* Oh Christine, if only Maman would place us together.

NATIVE SPEECH   Eric Overmyer

HUNGRY MOTHER's *underground radio station. "The studio is constructed from the detritus of Western Civilization. Outside, a darkening world. Dangerous. Always winter."* JANIS *(20s), a frail and lonely fan of* HUNGRY MOTHER's *(a male D.J.) has come in person to the studio to confide in him.*

JANIS: I don't feel good, Mother. I know you know what I'm—I know you feel the same
[HUNGRY MOTHER: I'm asking do you get it. Your asking me to help is the joke. I'm laughing. I'm larfing. You'd better larf

87

too.]

JANIS: I know you know how I feel.

[HUNGRY MOTHER: Not a glimmer.]

(Pause)

JANIS: I don't have furniture in my place. Nothing. A radio. I play the radio. Full blast. To keep the junkies away. They run through the building at night. Up and down the stairs. Fire escape. Rip the copper out of the walls. The wiring. There's no water. No light. They steal the stoves. The gas crawls up the wall. *(Slight pause)* I turn it up. Way up. Radio. Play it all night. Afraid to sleep. They run through the building all night. Scratch the walls. *(Slight pause)* I said that. *(Slight pause)* That's how I found you, Mother. One night. Down at the end of the dial. Before dawn. Strange voice. Cracked. Had a crack in it. Down at the end of the dial. Pain in it. *(Slight pause)* Thanks for turning up. You were so faint at first. When I first found you. Just a crackle. Clearer in winter than summer or spring . . . No, that's silly, but—my place is right across the park. I think the leaves must interfere? Anyway, lately—you're coming in clear as a bell. [. . .] Incredibly clear. What I am telling you. What I am trying to say. For more than a year now your voice has really made the difference to me, Mother.

(Pause) [. . .] *(Trying again, in a rush)* I felt you were lonely, you said you wanted letters, I could tell, I could tell you were, by your jokes, you were worried no one was listening, no one cared, no one was hearing you, so I wrote, I wrote you. I never dreamed, you know, of writing to a, public person, a stranger, I wouldn't you know, infringe on someone's privacy . . . so I was really distressed when you read my letters over the air . . . but in a way that was all right, it was okay, it was like you were listening, like you were answering. I never expected you to—that's why I signed my letters Desperate, . . .

NEW YORK SOCIAL LIFE   Laurie Anderson

This monologue is part of a large performance piece, UNITED
STATES, *performed by* LAURIE ANDERSON.

Well I was lying in bed one morning, trying to think of a good
reason to get up, and the phone rang and it was Geri and she said:
Hey, hi! How are you? What's going on? How's your work?

Oh fine. You know, just waking up but it's fine, it's going OK,
how's yours?

Oh a lot of work, you know, I mean, I'm trying to make some
money too. Listen, I gotta get back to it, I just thought I'd call to
see how you are . . .

And I said: Yeah, we should really get together next week. You
know, have lunch, and talk. And she says: Yeah, uh, I'll be in
touch, OK?

OK.

Uh, listen, take care.

OK. Take it easy.

Bye bye.

Bye now. And I get up, and the phone rings and it's a man from
Cleveland and he says: Hey, hi! How are you? Listen, I'm doing a
performance series and I'd like you to do something in it. Uh, you
know, you could make a little money. I mean, I don't know how I
feel about your work, you know, it's not really my style, it's kind
of trite, but listen, it's *just* my opinion, don't take it personally. So
listen, I'll be in town next week. I gotta go now, but I'll give you a
call, and we'll have lunch, and we can discuss a few things.

And I hang up and it rings again and I don't answer it and I go
out for a walk and I drop in at the gallery and they say: Hey, hi.
How are you?

Oh fine. You know.

How's your work going?

OK. I mean . . .

You know, it's not like it was in the sixties. I mean, those were the days, there's just no money around now, you know, survive, produce, stick it out, it's a jungle out there, just gotta keep working.

And the phone rings and she says: Oh excuse me, will you? Hey, hi! How are you? Uh huh. How's your work? *Good.* Well, listen, stick it out, I mean, it's not the sixties, you know, listen, I gotta go now, but, uh, lunch would be great.

Fine, next week? Yeah. Very busy now, but next week would be fine, OK? Bye bye.

Bye now.

And I go over to Magoo's, for a bite, and I see Frank and I go over to his table and I say:

Hey Frank. Hi, how are you? How's your work? Yeah, mine's OK too. Listen, I'm broke you know, but, uh, working . . . Listen, I gotta go now, uh, we should *really* get together, you know. Why don't you drop by sometime? Yeah, that would be great. OK. Take care.

Take it easy.

I'll see you.

I'll call you.

Bye now.

Bye bye.

And I go to a party and everyone's sitting around wearing these party hats and it's really awkward and no one can think of anything to say. So we all move around—fast—and it's: Hi! How are you? Where've you been? Nice to see you. Listen, I'm sorry I missed your thing last week, but we should really get together, you know, maybe next week. I'll call you. I'll see you.

Bye bye.

And I go home and the phone rings and it's Alan and he says: You know, I'm gonna have a show on, uh, cable TV and it's gonna be about loneliness, you know, people in the city who for whatever sociological, psychological, philosophical reasons just can't seem to communicate, you know, The Gap, The Gap, uh, it'll be a talk show and people'll phone in but we will say at the beginning of each program: Uh, listen, don't call in with your *personal* problems because we don't want to hear them.

And I'm going to sleep and it rings again and it's Mary and she says:

Hey, Laurie, how are you? Listen, uh, I just called to say hi . . . Uh, yeah, well don't worry. Uh, listen, just keep working. I gotta go now. I know it's late but we should really get together next week maybe and have lunch and talk and . . . Listen, Laurie, uh, if you want to talk before then, uh, I'll leave my answering machine on . . . and just give me a ring . . . anytime.

'NIGHT, MOTHER   Marsha Norman

The present. The living room/kitchen of a contemporary suburban house. JESSIE (40s) "is pale and vaguely unsteady physically." SHE has announced to HER mother that SHE is going to commit suicide, believing that by saying "no" to all HER options SHE will finally gain control of HER life. Here JESSIE tells MAMA that SHE is no longer a child and never became the person SHE thought SHE would be.

[MAMA: How can I let you go?]
JESSIE: You can because you have to. It's what you've always done.
[MAMA: You are my child!]
JESSIE: I am what became of your child. *(MAMA cannot answer)* I found an old baby picture of me. And it was somebody else, not me. It was somebody pink and fat who never heard of sick or lonely, somebody who cried and got fed, and reached up and got held and kicked but didn't hurt anybody, and slept whenever she wanted to, just by closing her eyes. Somebody who mainly just laid

there and laughed at the colors waving around over her head and chewed on a polka-dot whale and woke up knowing some new trick nearly every day and rolled over and drooled on the sheet and felt your hand pulling my quilt back up over me. That's who I started out and this is who is left. *(There is no self-pity here)* That's what this is all about. It's somebody I lost, all right, it's my own self. Who I never was. Or who I tried to be and never got there. Somebody I waited for who never came. And never will. So, see, it doesn't much matter what else happens in the world or in this house, even. I'm what was worth waiting for and I didn't make it. Me . . . who might have made a difference to me . . . I'm not going to show up, so there's no reason to stay, except to keep you company, and that's . . . not reason enough because I'm not . . . very good company. *(A pause)* Am I.

ONCE A CATHOLIC   Mary O'Malley

July 1957. A Catholic grammar (high) school for girls in Northwest London. MOTHER PETER, *a tall, stout, middle-aged, Irish teaching nun addresses the girls of Form 5A at the end of their summer term.* SHE *tells them what to expect next term.*

MOTHER PETER: When you come back in September you may wear nylon stockings and a smart grey skirt instead of a gymslip. But don't let me see any sign of lipstick or bits of old jewelry. Apart from a holy medal or a crucifix. Those of you going out into the world must remember that the devil will be beckoning to you from every corner. But you can just tell him to go to Hell because you're not going to be fooled by him and his wily ways. You're going to show him a shining example of Catholic purity. Always be modest in manner, in speech and in costume. You may often be puzzled when you see decent young men hovering around young women who wear scanty clothes and say provocative things. But you can be sure that such women are really the object of those men's secret contempt. Oh yes indeed. Remember that God made your body for himself. He lives in it and he may well want to use it for his own work later on when you marry, as a tabernacle for brand new life. All parts of the body are sacred but none so more than the parts connected with the mystery of motherhood. They should be treated with the greatest respect and guarded with absolute modesty. Scrupulous hygiene is of course vitally important and you need not imagine you are sinning when you sit in the bath and see yourself or touch yourself with the flannel. Just say a little prayer, think of Our Lady and remember that she had a body just like yours. Oh yes, and beware of indecent articles of news in what may otherwise appear to be innocent publications on sale in any shop. The *News of the World* is the one that springs most readily to mind. If you ever see the *News of the World* lying about on a bus or a train or any public place don't hesitate to tear it up. And the very same applies to the *Daily Worker*. The rotten old rag of the Communists. Rip it into pieces and let yourselves be seen ripping it up as an example to others. It's no easy task to live a good life in the adult world. We must take up our cross every day just like Our Blessed Lord and carry it with us wherever we go. And when God sends us any sickness or trouble we must accept it willingly and say "Thy will be done. I take this for my sins." And the best of luck to you. (SHE *makes the sign of the cross.*)

PASSIONE   Albert Innaurato

*The present. A small, cramped and old fashioned apartment in
South Philadelphia. FRANCINE (29), described as "immense,
clearly a good hundred pounds overweight. However, she is a very
beautiful fat woman." SHE works at the circus as the Fat Lady with
HER husband, LITTLE TOM, a clown. HER husband's mother
has just accused him of being a failure. FRANCINE agrees with
her but tries to console LITTLE TOM while gobbling a cream puff.*

[LITTLE TOM: Is she right? Am I a failure? Is there a
chance . . . maybe she's right?]

FRANCINE: Sure, she's right! You are a failure, Little Tom, no
two ways about it! Look! You're a wop in a Wasp culture, that's a
bad sign. When you had more hair it was greasy. That's a real bad
sign. And in a thin society where everybody gotta look like a
skeleton to be in, you're thirty, forty pounds overweight. My God,
Little Tom, you is failin' every test! Then you don't work at an
office. You dance around in the street. Things are lookin' worse
and worse! And just think—suppose I had you investigated! You
was in the mental ward of Methodist Hospital, right up there on
Broad Street, for attempted suicide! Oh my God! Have half this
cream puff, come on! And then, look what you got for a wife!
That's the last straw. A big fat blob. Is she chubby? Nah! Is she,
well on the fat side? Nah! She's fuckin' grotesque. Why ain't you
in that bathtub right now tryin' to die? Hanh? Tell me . . . Why,
if you was a decent American man of thirty, instead of a bum, you'd
go on a diet, get a divorce, and go to law school! And afta the
divorce, hanh? You find yourself a nice, thin blond girl who don't
give you no lip. Course, she won't give you no head neither . . .

94

PERSONALITY   Gina Wendkos & Ellen Ratner

The present. A New York City apartment. ELLEN *(30s) is single and very aware of it.* HER *overbearing Jewish mother never fails to remind* HER *of this fact. Here* ELLEN *indulges in a fantasy of what it would be like to be a "Hot Bitch."*

ELLEN: The thing I always wanted to be called was a HOT BITCH. There was something very sexy, very dirty, very Italian about that. I wanted it. I wanted to wake up one morning with some guy and hear him on the phone. Some guy named Jake or Rick. I wanted to lie in bed, leave the sheets draped so that only my thighs were covered. I'd lie there pretending to be asleep, but really I've got it arranged so I look takeable. Very takeable. I'll move my hair so that it covers the pillow but still shows my face and I'd lift up my hips so my waist looks smaller just like in the photos and I'll listen to this Jake or Rick of Tony guy on the phone, talking to one of his friends. "Hey, buddy, how ya doin'? Listen I've got this really hot bitch here. Yeah, she steams. Huh? Her name is Ellen, and she looks like a Sophia Loren type. One of those round hot Italians. Nah, met her on the street and I just wanted her. I couldn't stay away. So I went up to her and said I've never seen anyone like you. I've never smelled anyone like you, I've never wanted anyone like you, and she just looked at me and smiled. I knew I could touch her and I knew once I touched her I'd never leave. Yeah, she's really something else. I could get lost in her hair alone, it's so long and gets everywhere but I want my mouth on it." That's the kind of conversation I imagine. Then this Jake or Rick or Tony guy would come in and see me posed like that. Even if he knows it's arranged he'll like it. He'll come in and pull the sheet back and I'll stay still and he'll just look at me and I can feel his eyes, his wanting me, so I'll let out a little moan so he'll know I'm awake. *(Phone ring)* Fuck the personality for a minute. Sometimes I want to be wanted just for the way I walk.

95

PLAY MEMORY   Joanna M. Glass

*1947. Saskatchewan, Canada (prairie land). JEAN (20s-30s),
alone on the stage, reminisces about being twelve years old. SHE
describes the menial jobs SHE did to help make ends meet while
HER father, a violent alcoholic, was out of work.*

JEAN: I am twelve now. On Saturdays I work for Mrs. Sampson,
who has two little children. I take them with me, to the cellar,
where I do the laundry. They like it when the clothes have to be put
through the wringer. I let them do that while I take the wet pieces
outside, and hang them on the line to dry. Mrs. Sampson got very
mad at me last Saturday. It was thirty-eight degrees below zero, and
the sheets froze on the line. One of them cracked, broke in two right
in the middle, as I brought it through the door. Mrs. Sampson
hollered at me and said I was irresponsible. On Sundays I work
down at O'Malley's Fish and Chips. I weigh the chips on a scale
and then I put them into little plastic bags. There's an electric
machine, a hot iron clamp that seals the bags closed. It's a long
walk home, afterwards, but I don't take the trolley. My clothing
smells of fish and oil and I'm afraid there'll be someone I know, on
the trolley. My mother cooks in the kitchen at the Old Folks' Home.
She makes fifteen pies every day of the week, all by herself, with no
machines to help. In the evenings she sits and mends things, and
she remembers what it was like, in the old days, when I was little.
Last fall I was called into the counselor's office at school. *(Pause)* I
have—bladder trouble. She asked me if I could tell her something
about the changes that had occurred at our house. I remembered a
poem, by John Dryden, from an old book that belonged to my
Grandfather MacMillan. It described a time that was: "A very
merry, dancing, drinking/laughing, quaffing and unthinking time."
I told her it must have been like that, in the old days, when I was
little.

96

1947. London at night. A bed-sitter (studio apartment). SUSAN
*(20s), a bright and difficult woman, is working at a dreary office job
which* SHE *desperately wants to leave.* SHE *drinks hot cocoa and
talks to* HER *friend* ALICE. SUSAN *coldly describes the romantic
advances of a male co-worker, which may be real or just in* HER
imagination.

[ALICE: The boss?]
SUSAN: He has moved in. Or rather, more sinister still he has
removed the frosted glass between our two offices.
[ALICE: Really?]
SUSAN: I came in one morning and found the partition had gone.
I interpret it as the first step in a mating dance. I believe Medlicott
stayed behind one night, set his ledger aside, ripped off his tweed
suit, took up an axe, swung it at the partition, dropped to the floor,
rolled over in the broken glass till he bled, till his whole body
streamed blood, then he cleared up, slipped home, came back next
morning and waited to see if anything would be said. But I have
said nothing. And neither has he. He puts his head down and does
not lift it till lunch. I have to look across at his few strands of hair,
like seaweed across his skull. And I am frightened of what the next
step will be.
[ALICE: I can imagine.]
SUSAN: The sexual pressure is becoming intolerable. *(They
smile)* One day there was a condom in his trouser cuff. I tried to
laugh it off to myself, pretended he'd been off with some whore in
Limehouse and not bothered to take his trousers off, so that after the
event the condom had just absent-mindedly fallen from its place and
lodged alongside all the bus tickets and the tobacco and the raisins
and the paper-clips and all the rest of it. But I know the truth. It
was step two. And the dance has barely begun.

POSTCARDS Carol K. Mack

The present. A New York City apartment. JANE *(30s), a professional caterer, tells of the time* SHE *got catering stage fright.*

JANE: *(Drifting into recollection from present)* That night I made a daube for fifty. God, I was so nervous! I'd never made a daube before except one trial one for ... me and Tom. *(HER hands flop around a lot during the recall)* I was very, very nervous. As if I ... had a premonition of something bad ... I left him home with some paté and a couple of strawberry mousse and went to the party. The hostess made me nervous. She had told me at the start that she didn't want to do anything "nouvelle" because she thought it seemed too ... sparse ... at home. She said she didn't think that nouvelle would work because her friends were all tired of kiwi slices and she wanted a kind of "gloppy" feeling. *(SHE checks to see if* RIA *and* ISABEL *are following)* Like chunky cheese and peasant bread and daube ... O.K. so I am standing there in this kitchen, which is very white and the lights are so bright and I began to unwrap the containers I brought and I looked at this cold daube and it looked like shit, you know? It looked like an accident. Oh God. Ever since I started catering I get scared every time I start a party. I have this feeling that everyone there is going to die. It's like stage fright. I always get the same feeling ... that some can I used along the way had botulism. And *that* night all the guests will turn green and curl up on the floor. I see it: Lots of ambulances will have to come. When I do parties for a hundred I imagine a *fleet* of ambulances coming to take us all away. I always eat a small portion of everything so that I will die along with everyone else. I mean the idea that anyone would think *I* poisoned all the dinner guests is just too ... so I make sure that if there is a bacterium in the batch, I have some. The thing is that the night of the daube the feeling was very *intense.* I wanted desperately to go home! I thought it was just the normal stage fright of catering and not the premonition that it

98

turned out to be—this voice telling me to go home! Go
home . . . (SHE *has difficulty breathing.*)

THE REAL THING   Tom Stoppard

The present. London. The living room of a well-to-do family.
DEBBIE *(17) tells* HER *playwright father,* HENRY, *that* SHE *is
leaving home to move in with* HER *boyfriend, a fair ground
musician.* SHE *tells* HER *father, much to his amazement, some
candid things about* HER *attraction to sex.*

DEBBIE: Most people think *not* having it off is *fidelity.* They
think all relationships hinge in the middle. Sex or no sex. What a
fantastic range of possibilities. Like an on/off switch. Did she or
didn't she. By Henry Ibsen. Why would you want to make it such
a crisis?
[HENRY: I don't know, why would I?]
DEBBIE: It's what comes of making such a mystery of it. When I
was twelve I was obsessed. Everything was sex. Latin was sex.
The dictionary fell open at *meretrix,* a harlot. You could feel the
mystery coming off the word like musk. *Meretrix!* This was none
of your *amo, amas, amat,* this was a flash from the forbidden
planet, and it was everywhere. History was sex, French was sex,
art was sex, the Bible, poetry, penfriends, games, music, everything was sex except biology which was obviously sex but obviously not *really* sex, not the one which was secret and ecstatic and
wicked and a sacrament and all the things it was supposed to be but
couldn't be at one and the same time—I got that in the boiler room
and it turned out to be biology after all. That's what free love is free
of—propaganda.

RECKLESS   Craig Lucas

The present. A town called Springfield. POOTY *(20s), a*
paraplegic confined to a wheelchair and who pretends to be deaf and
dumb, finally speaks for the first time in the play. SHE *explains*
HER *motives to* RACHEL, *who has been living with* POOTY *and*
HER *husband* LLOYD.

POOTY: If you've ever worked with needy people, it doesn't
matter what their particular handicap, they can be blind, they can be
mentally ill, they can be disabled . . . I used to work with the
hearing impaired, teaching sign language. Almost immediately you
realize how easy it is to take their infirmity for granted in the sea of
so much need. Abnormality becomes normality. When I lost the
use of my legs, a friend drive me up here to Springfield to take a
look at this place where you work with the handicapped. I watched
the various physical therapists work with the patients and there was
one: I remember he was working with a quadraplegic. I thought he
was the most beautiful man I'd ever seen. A light shining out
through his skin. And I thought if I couldn't be with him I'd die.
But I knew I would just be one more crippled dame as far as he was
concerned, so my friend helped to get me registered as deaf and
disabled. I thought if I were somehow needier than the rest I would
get special attention. I realized soon enough—everyone get special
attention where Lloyd is concerned, but by then it was too late. He
was in love with me, with my honesty. He learned to sign; he told
me how he'd run away from a bad marriage and changed his name
so he wouldn't have to play child support. He got me a job at
Hands Across the Sea. I couldn't bring myself to tell him I had
another name and another life, that I'd run away too, because I
owed the government so much money and wasn't able to pay after
the accident . . . I believe in honesty. I believe in total honesty.
And I need him and he needs me to be the person he thinks I am and
I am that person, I really am that person. I'm a crippled deaf

girl—"Short and stout. Here is my wheelchair, here is my mouth."
[RACHEL: I'm not judging you.]
POOTY: When he goes out I scream and scream just to hear my voice. Noise. I recite poetry I remember from grade school, I babble, I talk to the television, I even call people on the phone and say it's a wrong number just to have a conversation. I'm afraid I'm going to open my mouth to scream one day and . . . *(SHE does: no sound. LLOYD re-enters.)*

THE RESURRECTION OF LADY LESTER
OyamO

1944. LADY DAY *(BILLIE HOLIDAY), the great black American blues singer, talks to the jazz musician* LESTER YOUNG *about the time* SHE *was locked up in a reform school and learned the meaning of fear.*

LADY DAY: But Prez, I need to feel free.
[LESTER: Free? We're free artists who find new sounds to tell old stories. We ain't slaves. I don't see no goddamn chains on you, woman. You must be dreaming.]
LADY DAY: The chains on me ain't got nothing to do with dreaming. Prez, it's hard for me to explain things; that's why I sing, I guess. But something happened to me once that I'll never forget. When they locked me up in that girls' reform school, my first cellmate what this girl named Emma, a tall, black skin country girl, and she was a mean, vicious bitch and damn near strong as a man. They put her there for castratin' one of her uncles with a butcher knife. Soon as I step in the door, she jumped up and smacked me and told me how she hated my guts and I better do everything she said or she'd cut off my titties. Prez, I swear before my Saviour, I peed in my bloomers. I was so afraid I didn't move even when the water was running down my leg. I just stood there

crying and trembling for a long time, afraid to move unless she said move. When I looked up at her, she was sitting back all cool, smiling. Then she got polite, even nice, let me sit down, gave me a chocolate bar, talked about herself and where she came from. She sounded so nice and was treating me so good, that I didn't think it would be no problem if I got up and changed my bloomers. Soon as I stood up, she punched me in the stomach, knocked me over the bed. I learned quick. As long as I did what pleased her, she was polite, gentle, loving, fun even. But if I did anything, even something accidental, that displeased her, she'd beat the living daylights out me or she'd starve me, or she'd make me stand alone in a corner during recreation periods, or something. Prez, this world ain't never let me forget what that feels like. I mean, I named you Prez because you're the best, just like Roosevelt, but you still colored and no matter how great you blow that tenor, if you don't do what ole marsa "ask" you to do in this place, you liable to be hung out to dry. You all tell me I'm a great singer, but no matter how good I sing, I'm still locked up in a small corner of everybody's mind, regardless to who marsa is.

RIPEN OUR DARKNESS   Sarah Daniels

The present. TARA (30s-40s), the wife of an English psychiatrist, delivers this monologue to the audience. In it SHE reacts to the sexual pressures and constrictions of being married to MARSHALL.)

TARA: I don't believe you've met my husband, Marshall, yet. He's a psychiatrist. Yes, quite a conversation-stopper, isn't it? People are always intrigued to know about the ins and outs of his home life. You know, like the fascination we all have about clergymen who embezzle the collection or policemen who murder prostitutes, but unfortunately, Marshall's typically sane. Of course, he has his little routine and rituals. And as for sex, well, my dear, you can imagine how paranoid psychiatrists are about that. When we were first married we used to go to the Greek islands for our holidays and I adored making love on the beach but Marsh, poor love, was absolutely, obsessionally, preoccupied with the fear of getting a grain of sand under his foreskin. He thinks that magazines like *Forum* are where it's at. That's where he got the idea to try and train me to relax my throat muscles to perfect my fellatio performance. Don't misunderstand me, it's not that I don't enjoy risking my life but I do make it a little rule that I derive some pleasure from it. We've got two children and Marsh worked himself into a state of psychosis in case they were born with one testis too few or too many but despite all fears they're terribly normal. Oh, yes, they're both boys—pigs—don't tell me, darling, I've tried them with the handicraft classes, cookery, the lot, until I've literally pulled my hair out—still, I must be fair, they're not all bad. The youngest, he's eight, burnt the Scout hut down last week, so there's hope yet.

Of course, we have someone who takes the tedium out of housework—you know, our little treasure—does that sound exploitative? Frankly, I'm bored out of my mind and if I had to do irksome grotto chores I'd go completely off my head.

I love going to the pictures in the afternoon—it's so common.

Marshall is trying to sue Ken Russell because it was after I saw *Women in Love* I suffered my little bout of kleptomania. Anyway, you know that bit in the film where that other woman smashes a vase over that prick's head—are we still allowed to say "prick"? Are we still allowed to say "head"? God, this modifying of manmade linguistics has got us all confused. Anyhow, to cut a long story short, I lifted a Baccarat paperweight from Liberty's. Quite what I had in mind I don't know but one of our solicitor friends got me off the hook by saying I'd had a bad day.

Between you and I, Marsh has begged me to divorce him. Why

103

should I? I don't want to live in some pokey little flat where some social worker might try and certify me for being batty. No thanks. I like being posh.

Don't listen to this live without men rot. The way forward is to use them and have some fun.

ROAD   Jim Cartwright

The present. A depressed block of flats in the north of England where poverty and unemployment reign. VALERIE (20s-30s), alone in a scruffy dressing gown and sad nightie, sits on a chair in the middle of HER *kitchen smoking.* VAL *is waiting for* HER *drunken deadbeat husband to return home.* SHE *describes a life that is dreary and marginal.*

VALERIE: I'm fed up of sitting here waiting for him, he'll be another hundred years at this rate. What a life: get up, feed every baby in the house. Do everything else I can, without cash. While he drinks, drinks it, drinks it, and shoves nothing my way except his fat hard hands in bed at night. Rough dog he is. Big rough heavy dog. Dog with sick in its fur. He has me pulling my hair out. Look at my hair, it's so dry. So sadly dried. I'd cry but I don't think tears would come. And there's nothing worse than an empty cry. It's like choking. Why do we do it? Why do I stay? Why the why why? You can cover yourself in questions and you're none the wiser cause you're too tired to answer. Always scrimping and scraping. He just takes the Giro and does what he wants with it. Leaves a few pounds on the table corner sometimes, sometimes. But you never know when and if you ask him he chops you one. That's why I have to borrow, borrow off everyone. I am like a boney rat going here, going there, trying to sniffle something out. They help me, though I'll bet you they hate me really. Despise me really. Because I'm always there an' keep asking asking and they can't say no. They just open their purses, and I says, thank you, thank you a thousand times till we all feel sick. God I can't wait till the kids are older then I can send them. He'll come in soon. Pissed drunk through. Telling me I should do more about the place. Eating whatever's in the house. Pissing and missing the bog. Squeezing the kids too hard. Shouting then sulking. Then sleeping all deep and smelly; wrapped over and over in the blankets. Drink's a bastard. Drink's a swilly brown bastard. A smelling stench at sea. And he's the captain with his bristles wet through. Swallowing and throwing, swallowing and throwing white brown water all over me. Oh what am I saying, it's a nightmare all this. I blame him then I don't blame him. It's not his fault there's no work. He's such a big man, he's nowhere to put himself. He looks so awkward and sad at the sink, the vacuum's like a toy in his hand. When he's in all day he fills up the room. Like a big wounded animal, moving about, trying to find his slippers, clumsy with the small things of the house, bewildered. I see this. I see the poor beast in the wrong world. I see his eyes sad and low. I see him as the days go on, old damp sacks one on top of another. I see him, the waste. The human waste of the land. But I can't forgive him. I can't forgive the cruel of the big fucking heap. The big fucking clumsy heap. *(SHE startles herself with what SHE's saying; nearly cries)* He's so big and hunched and ugly. *(Holding back)* Oh my man. *(SHE chokes)* I hate him now, and I didn't used to. I hate him now, and I don't want to. *(SHE cries)* Can we not have before again, can we not? *(Crying)* Can we not have before again. *(SHE looks out, manic and abrupt)* Can we not?

ROCKABY   Samuel Beckett

W = *Woman in chair.*
V = *Her recorded voice.*

Face up on W *in rocking chair facing front downstage slightly off
center audience left.*

Long pause.

W: More.

Pause. Rock and voice together.

V: till in the end
     the day came
     in the end came
     close of a long day
     when she said
     to herself
     whom else
     time she stopped
     time she stopped
     going to and fro
     all eyes
     all sides
     so in the end
     close of a long day
     went back in
     in the end went back in
     saying to herself
     whom else
     time she stopped
     time she stopped
     going to and fro

time she went and sat
at her window
quiet at her window
facing other windows
so in the end
close of a long day
in the end went and sat
went back in and sat
at her window
let up the blind and sat
quiet at her window
only window
facing other windows
other only windows
all eyes
all sides
high and low
for another
at her window
another like herself
a little like
another living soul
one other living soul
at her window
gone in like herself
going back in
in the end
close of a long day
saying to herself
whom else
time she stopped
time she stopped
going to and fro

time she went and sat
at her window
quiet at her window
only window
facing other windows
other only windows
all eyes
all sides
high and low
for another
another like herself
a little like
another living soul
one other living soul

Together: echo of "living soul," coming to rest of rock, faint fade of light.

Long pause.

THE SEARCH FOR SIGNS OF INTELLIGENT LIFE IN THE UNIVERSE
Jane Wagner

This piece is one of a series of monologues written for and performed by LILY TOMLIN. TRUDY, *an eccentric and talkative bag lady, presents* HER *views on life as* SHE *waits to meet* HER *friends from outer space.*

TRUDY: Here we are, standing on the corner of
"Walk, Don't Walk."
You look away from me, tryin' not to catch my eye,
but you didn't turn fast enough, *did* you?

You don't like my *ras*py voice, do you?
I got this *ras*py voice
'cause I have to yell all the time
'cause nobody around here ever
LISTENS to me.

You don't like that I scratch so much; yes, and excuse me,
I scratch so much
'cause my neurons are
on *fire*

And I admit my smile is not at its Pepsodent best
'cause I think my
caps must've somehow got
osteo*porosis.*

And if my eyes seem to be twirling around like fruit flies—
the better to see you with, my dears!

Look at me,
you mammalian-brained LUNKHEADS!
I'm not just talking to myself, I'm talking to you, too.
And to you
and you
and you
and you and you and you!

I know what you're thinkin'; you're thinkin' I'm crazy.
You think I give a hoot? You people
look at my shopping bags,
call me crazy 'cause I save this junk. What should we call the
ones who
buy it?

It's my belief we all, at one time or another,

secretly ask ourselves the question,
"Am *I* crazy?"
In my case, the answer came back: A resounding
YES!

You're thinkin': How does a person know if they're crazy
or not? Well, sometimes you don't know. Sometimes you
can go through life suspecting you *are*
but never really knowing for sure. Sometimes you know for sure
'cause you got so many people tellin' you you're crazy
that it's your word against everyone else's.

Another sign is when you see life so clear sometimes
you black out.
This is your typical visionary variety
who has flashes of insight
but can't get anyone to listen to 'em
'cause their insights make 'em sound so *crazy!*

In my case, the symptoms are subtle
but unmistakable to the trained eye. For instance,
here I am,
standing at the corner of "Walk, Don't Walk,"
waiting for these aliens from outer space to show up.
I call that crazy, don't you? If I were sane,
I should be waiting for the light like everybody else.

They're late
as usual.

You'd think,
as much as they know about time travel,
they could be on time *once* in a while.

I could kick myself.

110

I told 'em I'd meet 'em on the corner of "Walk, Don't Walk"
'round lunchtime.
Do they even know what "lunch" means?
I doubt it.

And "'round." Why did I say "'round"? Why wasn't I more
specific? This is so typical of what I do.

Now they're probably stuck somewhere in time, wondering
what I meant by
"'round lunchtime." And when they get here, they'll be
dying to know what "lunchtime" means. And when they
find out it means going to Howard Johnson's for fried
clams, I wonder, will they be just a bit let down?

I dread having to explain
tartar sauce.

This problem of time just points out
how far apart we really are.
See, our ideas about time and space are different
from theirs. When we think of time, we tend to think of
clock radios, coffee breaks, afternoon naps, leisure time,
halftime activities, parole time, doing time, Minute Rice, instant tea,
mid-life crisis, that time of the month, cocktail hour.
And if I should suddenly
mention *space*—aha! I bet most of you thought of your
closets. But when they think of time and space, they really think of
Time and Space.

They asked me once my thoughts on infinity and I told 'em
with all I had to think about, infinity was not on my list
of things to think about. I t could be time on an ego trip,
for all I know. After all, when you're pressed for time,
infinity may as well

not be there.
They said, to them, infinity is
time-released time.

Frankly, infinity doesn't affect
me personally one way or the other.

You think too long about infinity, you could go
stark raving mad.
But I don't ever want to sound negative about going crazy.
I don't want to overromanticize it either, but frankly,
goin' crazy was the *best* thing ever happened to me.
I don't say it's for everybody;
some people couldn't cope.

But for me it came at a time when nothing else seemed to be
working. I got the kind of madness Socrates talked about,
"A divine release of the soul from the yoke of
custom and convention." I refuse to be intimidated by
reality anymore.
After all,what is reality anyway? Nothin' but a
collective hunch. My space chums think reality was once a
primitive method of
crowd control that got out of hand.
In my view, it's absurdity dressed up
in a three-piece business suit.

I made some studies, and
reality is the leading cause of stress amongst those in
touch with it. I can take it in small doses, but as a lifestyle
I found it too confining.
It was just too needful;
it expected me to be there for it *all* the time, and with all
I have to do—

I had to let something go.

Now, since I put reality on a back burner, my days are
jam-packed and fun-filled. Like some days, I go hang out
around Seventh Avenue; I love to do this old joke:
I wait for some music-loving tourist from one of the hotels
on Central Park to go up and ask someone,
"How do I get to Carnegie Hall?"
Then I run up and yell,
"Practice!"
The expression on people's faces is priceless. I never
could've done stuff like that when I was in my *right* mind.
I'd be worried people would think I was *crazy*.
When I think of the fun I missed,
I try not to be bitter.

See, the human mind is kind of like . . .

a piñata. When it breaks open,
there's a lot of surprises inside. Once you get the piñata
perspective, you see that losing your mind
can be a peak experience.

I was not always a bag lady, you know.
I used to be a designer and creative consultant. For big
companies!
Who do you think thought up the color scheme
for Howard Johnson's?
At the time, nobody was using
orange and aqua
in the same room together.
With fried clams.

Laugh tracks:
I gave TV sitcoms the idea for canned laughter.

I got the idea, one day I heard voices
and no one was there.

Who do you think had the idea to package panty hose
in a plastic goose egg?
One thing I personally don't like about panty hose:
When you roll 'em down to the ankles the way I like 'em, you
can't walk too good. People seem amused, so what's a little
loss of dignity? You got to admit:
It's a look!

The only idea I'm proud of—

my umbrella hat. Protects against sunstroke, rain and
muggers. For *some* reason, muggers steer clear of people
wearing umbrella hats.

So it should come as no shock . . . I am now creative consultant
to these aliens from outer space. They're a kinda cosmic
fact-finding committee. Amongst other projects, they've been
searching all over for Signs of Intelligent Life.

It's a lot trickier than it sounds.

We're collecting all kinds of data
about life here on Earth. We're determined to figure out,
once and for all, just what the hell it all means.
I write the data on these Post-its and then we study it.
Don't worry, before I took the consulting job, I gave 'em my whole
psychohistory.

I tole 'em what drove *me* crazy was my *last* creative consultant job,
with the Ritz Cracker mogul, Mr. Nabisco. it was my job to come
up with snack inspirations to increase sales. I got this idea to give
Cracker Consciousness to the entire planet.

I said, "Mr. Nabisco, sir! You could be the first to sell the concept
of munching to the Third World. We got an untapped market here!
These countries got millions and millions of people don't even know
where their next *meal* is *coming* from.
So the idea of eatin' *between* meals is somethin' just never
occurred to 'em!"

I heard myself sayin' *this!*

Must've been when I went off the deep end.
I woke up in the nuthouse. They were hookin' me up.
One thing they don't tell you about shock treatments, for
months afterwards you got
flyaway hair. And it used to *be* my best feature.

See, those shock treatments gave me new electrical circuitry
(frankly, I think one of the doctors' hands must've been wet).
I started having these time-space continuum shifts, I guess
you'd call it. Suddenly, it was like my central nervous system
had a patio addition out back.
Not only do I have a linkup to extraterrestrial
channels. I also got a hookup with humanity as a whole.
Animals and plants, too. I used to talk to plants all the time;
then, one day, they started talking back. They said,
"Trudy, shut up!"

I got like this . . .

built-in Betamax in my head. Records anything.
It's like somebody's using my brain to dial-switch
through humanity. I pick up signals that seem to transmit
snatches of people's lives.
My umbrella hat works as a satellite dish. I hear this
sizzling sound like white noise. Then I know it's
trance time.

That's how I met my space chums. I was in one of my trances,
watching a scene from someone's life, and I suddenly sense
others were there
watching with me.

Uh-oh.
I see this skinny
punk kid.
Got hair the color of
Froot Loops and she's wearin' a T-shirt says "Leave Me Alone."
There's a terrible family squabble going on.
If they're listening to each other,
they're all gonna get their feelings hurt.

I see glitches—
Now I see this dark-haired actress
on a Broadway stage. I know her. I see her all the time outside the
Plymouth Theater, Forty-fifth Street.

SHIVAREE   William Mastrosimone

*The present. An apartment in a Southern city. SHIVAREE (20s),
an American girl who works as a belly dancer, has just climbed over
the balcony into CHANDLER's apartment. This is their first
meeting. SHE tells HIM about the thrill of pleasing other people
with HER dancing.*

SHIVAREE: Well, sport, you can dance for dance and get a flat
rate, or you can dance for tips and get what you get. Like after
dancin' at the Hyatt last night, seven sheiks from Dubai approach
me and said they was throwin' some highbrow shindig up in their
suite, would I grace their company with the dance, salam alekum,
the whole bit, and I says, Hell yeah, and I walks in and it looks like

a sheet sale, all kinds of Mideastern folk jabberin' and the musicians go big for some Guazi tune and I let loose my stuff. I do veil work where I put myself in this envelope like a little chrysalis in a gossamer cocoon listenin' to the beat of my heart, and then I break out with hip shimmies and shoulder rolls and bell flutter, mad swirls, Byzantine smiles and half-closed eyes, and my hands are cobras slitherin' on air, hoods open and I'm Little Egypt, Theodora, Nefertiti, and Salome, all in one skin, and these before me was Solomon and Herod and Caesar and Tutankhamen shoutin' Ayawah, Shivaree, Ayawah, which roughly means, Go for it, little darlin'—and this young sheik he's clappin' hands to my zills, and he rolls up this hundred dollar bill and tries to slip it in my clothes, which makes me stop dancin', which makes the musicians stop, and there's this hush when I fling that hundred dollar bill on the rug, and it gets so quiet you could hear a rat tiptoe on cotton, and I says, Look here, sucker, I'm a dancer, and I'm moved by Ishtar, Aphrodite, Venus, Isis, Astarte, and Rickee Lee Jones, all of them sultry ladies of the East. I am the goddess of the feathery foot, and I only take orders from the moon. Direct. I have turned dives into temples, cadavers into footstompers, drunks into believers, and Tuesday night into Sunday mornin' gospel-time, and I don't take tips. It ain't proper to tip a goddess. And I starts to leave in a huff, and the young sheik comes to 'pologize, asks me to Arabia, he would take care o' everything, and then I know he's talkin' about the even more ancient horizontal-dance of the harem girl, and I says, Tell me, sheik, you got biscuits 'n gravy over there? And he says, What's biscuits and gravy? And I walks out sayin', See there, sheik, you're living a deprived life,—And that's m'story bub.

The present. A city bar full of entertainers, waiting for a "break."
NATALIE (20s), an unemployed black performer, thinks about
what it would be like if SHE were white.

NATALIE: today i'm gonna be a white girl/ i'll retroactively wake myself up/ ah low & behold/ a white girl in my bed/ but first i'll haveta call a white girl i know to have some more accurate information/ what's the first thing white girls think in the morning/ do they get up being glad they ain't niggahs/ do they remember mama/ or worry abt gettin to work/ do they work?/ do they play isdora & wrap themselves in sheets & go tip toeing to the kitchen to make maxwell house coffee/ oh i know/ the first thing a white girl does in the morning is fling her hair/

So now i'm done with that/ i'm gonna water my plants/ but am i a po white trash white girl with a old jellyjar/ or am i a sophisticated & protestant suburbanite with 2 valiums slugged awready & a porcelain water carrier leading me up the stairs strewn with heads of dolls & nasty smellin white husband person's underwear/ if i was really protected from the niggahs/ i might go to early morning mass & pick up a tomato pie on the way home/ so i cd eat it during the young & the restless. in williams arizona as a white girl/ i cd push the navaho women outta my way in the supermarket & push my nose in the air so i wdnt haveta smell them. coming from bay ridge on the train i cd smile at all the black & puerto rican people/ & hope they cant tell i want them to go back where they came from/ or at least be invisible.

i'm still in my kitchen/ so i guess i'll just have to fling my hair again & sit down. i shd pinch my cheeks to bring the color back/ i wonder why the colored lady hasn't arrived to clean my house yet/ so i cd go to the beauty parlor & sit under a sunlamp to get some more color back/ it's terrible how god gave those colored women such clear complexions/ it take em years to develop wrinkles/ but beauty can be bought & flattered into the world.

as a white girl on the street/ i can assume since i am a white girl on the streets/ that everyone notices how beautiful i am/ especially lil black & caribbean boys/ they love to look at me/ i'm exotic/ no one in their families looks like me/ poor things. if i waz one of those white girls who loves one of those grown black fellas/ i cd say with my eyes wide open/ totally sincere/ oh i didnt know that/ i cd say i didt know/ i cant/ i dont know how/ cuz i'ma white girl & i dont have to do much of anything.

all of this is the fault of the white man's sexism/ oh how i loathe tight-assed thin-lipped pink white men/ even the football players lack a certain relaxed virility. that's why my heroes are either just like my father/ who while he still cdnt speak english knew enough to tell me how the niggers shd go back where they came from/ or my heroes are psychotic faggots who are white/ or else they are/ oh/ you know/ colored men.

being a white girl by dint of my will/ is much more complicated than i thought it wd be/ but i wanted to try it cuz so many men like white girls/ white men/ black men/ latin men/ jewish men/ asians/ everybody. so i thought if i waz a white girl for a day i might understand this better/ after all gertrude stein wanted to know abt the black women/ alice adams wrote *thinking abt billie*/joyce carol oates has three different black characters all with the same name/ i guess cuz we are underdeveloped individuals or cuz we are all the same/ at any rate i'm gonna call this thinkin abt white girls/ cuz helmut newton's awready gotta book called *white women*/ see what i mean/ that's a best seller/ one store i passed/ hadda sign said/

```
┌─────────────────────┐
│   WHITE WOMEN       │
│   SOLD OUT          │
└─────────────────────┘
```

it's this kinda pressure that forces us white girls to be so absolutely pathological abt the other women in the world/ who now that they're not all servants or peasants want to be considered beautiful too. we simply krinkle our hair/ learn to dance the woogie dances/ slant our eyes with make-up or surgery/ learn spanish & claim argentinian background/ or as a real trump card/ show up looking like a real white girl. you know all western civilization depends on us/

STEAMING   Nell Dunn

The present. London. The women's side of a municipal steam bath. JOSIE (34) works as a topless dancer. Never quite able to make ends meet and desperate for love and romance, SHE relies on a series of passing lovers. Make-up and clothes are important to HER. And HER fifteen-year-old son has been placed in a reform school. Here JOSIE talks about the problems with HER current man.

JOSIE: *(Beginning to undress)* Yes and you know what? I've got me rollers in me hair, a long nightgown, long pink socks, the top of a pair of pyjamas and he still wants to fuck me! He shouts at me, "Take them off now!" He shouts in his German accent, "Take them off now!" And he likes to rip them off! And he really hurt ripping off my suspenders—brand new they were and I can't wear them now. *(As SHE undresses SHE admires herself in the mirror)* He hasn't got any friends—he never does anything exciting, he doesn't even want a car. It's automatic, his life—get up, get dressed, go to work, come home, have dinner, have a wash, watch telly, have a screw—that' the only thing he does like, sex, every night, loads of it—I'm even getting sick of that, and you know me ... *(gloomy)* ... I love sex!

There you are—so I'm stuck with my Jerry—he's sat there and he's said, "I'm bored". "Oh, so you're bored are you?"—and I picks up his shirt—"Well, I'll give you something to do"—and I've taken his shirt ... *(SHE does the gestures)* ... and one by one I've twisted off the buttons—one, two, three, four—"There you

120

are," I said, "Now go and sew those back on, that'll give you something to do!" Well, he's just looked at me—stared at me—like this . . . (SHE *gives a mad cold stare*) . . . then he says, "Do you like snow?" "Not much," I says. And he goes to the cupboard and gets out this big bag of flour and scatters it all over me kitchen—it's gone everywhere—well, I just laughed, but he didn't laugh, he just sat and stared at me while I cleaned it up! What does he want out of life—you tell me, I mean we're not little kids, so what does he want? There's no joy there—I got this beautiful second-hand bench and I've painted it up—he didn't like it. I see this beautiful red dress—bright red with a red scarf to match—£40—that's the dress I want, I says—he doesn't buy it. Jean can get anything off a man . . . what's the matter with me?

(JOSIE *is now naked and arranging* HER *bed.*)

STEVIE   Hugh Whitemore

1950s. London. The living room of a cluttered suburban house.
STEVIE SMITH *(40s) was a leading English poet, who led an extremely suburban life.* SHE *was a small, hunched, bird-like woman, with quick gestures and the spontaneity of a child.* SHE *dressed sensibly and lived with a maiden aunt all* HER *life. From an early age* SHE *had contemplated suicide. Here* SHE *talks about that and about how* SHE *has "never fitted in."*

STEVIE: No, I never fitted in. Like the little boy in the commercial class who was told to try his hand at commercial correspondence. "Dear Sir," he wrote, "Sadly we see our customers falling away from us, but I hope that we shall always be friends. And so, with love." They soon taught him business language, oh yes, he was soon corrected. But not me, not Stevie, I was always slightly out of step. I used to think I should've been a pirate or something, a North Sea pirate. We're all seafaring men in our family, after all, even my poor father. It was good for me, though, the office routine, I needed the discipline. If I'd never had to work I'd have become some sort of invalidish person and never done any writing; it was exile from domesticity that produced my poems. I enjoyed a lot of it too, office life, oh yes. I loved the stock exchange language they used, with its curious religious undertones: conversion, redemption, pegged at sixty. Marvellous! It wasn't a taxing job either, far from it. I used to sit in my tiny office, writing poems and books, and asking my friends round for tea and hot buttered toast. My boss never complained, never, never so much as gave me a reproachful glance, he was very kind. *(SHE chuckles)* He used to advise me about stocks and shares. "Have you anything in Gossards?" he'd say. "If you've anything in Gossards, then sell." My word, how we laughed. Dear Sir Frank, I can see him now: walking past my office door in dark, dark mourning clothes and a dark, dark top hat. He was forever going to funerals. "Another good man buried," he'd say, and walk on with sombre tread.

(Brief pause. SHE rises. The smile fades from HER face)

There's not much to say about the suicide business; it's something I'd rather forget. It's too painful, too much remorse. Not because of the act itself, no, one regrets the pain one inflicts on other people. Aunt. Sir Frank, My friends at the office. It shouldn't have happened there, not like that, poor Sir Frank was dreadfully upset. Upset, but not surprised, I doubt very much whether he was greatly surprised. "I'm rather disturbed about this death feeling in your poems, Stevie," he said to me once. He knew. Oh yes, he knew.

(SHE is silent for a moment; HER head bows forward.)

The time is now. The place is where we are. CHERYL *(28) is married to* MARK *(28): "an ex-marine, Viet Nam vet, artist, lover, father." Their marriage has not been an easy one. The war has left* MARK *unsettled. In this "spaghetti story,"* CHERYL *reveals the tensions and pressures they share.*

CHERYL: I hate to cook. Probably because he likes to cook. I hate to cook. I don't now how to cook, and I hate it. Mark does this spaghetti dinner once a year. Has he ever told you about that? Holy Christ!
[MARK: EXCUSE ME. *(Leaves.)*]
CHERYL: Every day before Thanksgiving Mark does a spaghetti dinner, and this is a traditional thing. This is the one traditional bone Mark has in his body, and I'd like to break it. He has 20-45 people come to this thing. He makes ravioli, lasagne, spaghetti, meatballs, three different kinds of spaghetti sauces: shrimp, plain, meat sauce. Oh, he makes gnocci! He makes his own noodles! And it's good. He's a damn good cook for Italian food. But you can imagine what I go through for three weeks for that party to feed forty people. Sit-down dinner. He insists it's a sit-down dinner. So here I am running around with no time to cook with him. I'm trying to get enough shit in my house to feed forty people sit-down dinner. We heated the porch last year because we did not have enough room to seat forty people. And I run around serving all these slobs, and this is the first year he's really charged anyone. And we lose on it every year. I mean, we lose, first year we lost $300. This dinner is a $500 deal. I'm having a baby this November, and if he thinks he's having any kind of spaghetti dinner, he can get his butt out of here. I can't take it.

Pizzas! He makes home-made pizzas. You should see my oven. Oh my God! There's pizza-shit everywhere. Baked on. And when it's over with, he just gets up and walks out. He's just done. The

123

clean-up is no big deal to him. He won't even help. He rolls up the carpets for this dinner. People get smashed! He's got wine everywhere, red wine. It has to be red so if it get on my rugs, my rugs are ruined and my couch is ruined. I've just said it so many times I hate it. He knows I hate it. My brother brought over some speed to get me through that night. My brother, Jack, who is a capitalist—intelligent—makes me sick. Never got into drugs. Was too old. Missed that whole scene. But he now has speed occasionally on his bad day, you know, drink, two drinks one night, speed to get him through the day. Business man. He brought me some speed to get me through the night cause he knew what a basket case I'd be. And then Mark goes and invites my family. And they're the last people I want to see at this. Sure, they love it. I mean, they all sit around and they stuff themselves to death. I'm not kidding! It is one big stuffing feast. The first time, the first spaghetti dinner we had was right after Danny was born. Danny's baby book got torn up. I had to start a whole new one. Mark's crazy friends. Drunk. Broken dishes everywhere. I'm not kidding! It's just a disaster. Spaghetti on the walls. Spaghetti pots dropped in the kitchen. Spaghetti all over the sink. That's why I ask him. I go: "Why." "It's traditional. I have to do this every year." It was three years ago he started. Tradition my ass. I'm telling you. I mean, he wonders why I can't sleep with him sometimes. Because I just work up such a hate for him inside that *(Mark re-enters)* I'm a perfectionist. My house has to be this way, and before I go to sleep, I'll pick up after him. I'm constantly picking up after him. Christ Almighty! In the morning, if he comes in late, he's read the newspaper and there's newspaper all over the room. He *throws* it when he's done with it. I've broken toes on his shoes. I broke *this* toe on his shoe. He always leaves his shoes right out in walking space. Every morning I trip on either his tennis or his good shoes. Whichever pair he doesn't have on. He's so inconsiderate of other people. He's so selfish, he's so self-centered. And this is what I tell him. I just tired of it. He's so selfish. Because this spaghetti dinner just ruins me. Baby or no baby, it just completely ruins me. And he's showing off his, his wonderful cooking that he does once a year. And I suppose that is why I hate cooking.

TERMINAL BAR   Paul Selig

The near future. The Terminal Bar, a nearly abandoned club in New York's Broadway area. Winter. MARTINELLE (25) sits alone. SHE is vaguely attractive, wearing a fake fur chubby, a mini-skirt, and sequined platform shoes. It is not hard to guess HER profession. SHE is fiddling with a radio which SHE has stolen from a "Crazy Eddie" discount store. SHE talks to someone off-stage about how SHE got the radio.

MARTINELLE: So there I am, standin' in the ruins of the Crazy Eddie Christmas window holding on to this T.V. for dear life, an' I am dealing with this PERSON who is trying to pry it outa my arms. So I tell him, "What do I look like to you that allows for you to treat me in such a manner? I'm no refugee. You don't see me dragging my mattress along the highway." But he wasn't buying. So I say, "YOU take the radio an' give ME the damn T.V." . . . Charlie? You get through to Staten Island or you still loving yourself in the mirror? Anyways, I told this guy he'd look real sharp walking around the streets with a radio. He said it was a basic look an' he was not a basic person. I told him to look on the positive. Fact that anybody's still walkin' the streets at all is cause for a party. "Radio'd add a bit of class," I said. "Like being in your own parade." The he says to ME, "All's fair in love an' looting," an' he dances out the window with the freakin' tube . . . I'm not getting any stations on this. How's that for fun, huh Charlie? I spray painted lips on the hole in the wall. It's a big kiss from me to you . . . Charlie?

125

'TIL THE BEATLES REUNITE   Len Berkman

*The present. A home shared by the recently divorced CHIP and his
friend DAVID, who, together with their daughters, have formed a
new family. CHIP's daughter WILDFLOWER (15) (real name
RUTH) and DAVID's daughter "Q-TIP" (13) (real name PIPER)
have also formed a close attachment. Q-TIP wonders why WILD-
FLOWER's mother can't marry her father and come to live with
them under the same roof. WILDFLOWER, in the gentlest way
SHE can, tries to explain what SHE has figured out about the relationship between their fathers.*

WILDFLOWER: My father loves your father. He wants to lie in
your father's bed. I don't have proof but I feel it in my bones. I
hear such things happen.

(A silence as SHE takes in Q-Tips response)

I don't think men can do anything with each other, but I've heard
they can wish they could. And there are lots of people who throw
up just at the idea. So if your daydream came true and my mother
married your father, it would make things complicated.

(Another moment to sense Q-Tip's understanding)

Sometimes you walk into a room with my dad and yours and you
feel—I don't know—like you're interrupting. Not like you always
interrupt with adults but like it used to be with my mom and dad in
the good days. Even when it's just they're in the middle of an argument, you know you're interrupting and you're sort of out of
place in your very own home.

(SHE has to pause again, overwhelmed)

It's not a secret. Just a guess. I wish it *was* a secret. When
mom and dad used to sleep in separate rooms—almost like your dad
and my dad now—I'd stay awake hoping I'd hear one of them
tiptoeing over to the other. Lucky for me their doors had squeaky
hinges. During the months things got better, just before they
collapsed, I'd doze off to the music of those squeaks. When *I*

126

become a mother, that's what my husband and I will share: a single bedroom with one squeaky door. But you know what I'll do? I'll tie a rope from the doorknob to our bedpost. And my husband and I will pull on that rope all through the night. *(Pause)* We'll have the best rested children in the world.

TOM AND VIV   **Michael Hastings**

1932. An upper middle class house, London. ROSE *(70s) the mother of* VIV, *T.S. Eliot's wife, has reluctantly agreed that* HER *daughter should be institutionalized. All* HER *life* ROSE *has tried to protect* VIV, *and hide her mental condition. Here* SHE *wistfully remembers* VIV's *childhood.*

ROSE: There always have been doctors. All her life. And at school. Oh my—she was bright. First at piano. First to audition for the Royal Ballet School. To fail there was an honor. And languages. An impeccable accent. So much so, when school party went to Paris, strangers stopped and were astonished. Such a good school, too. And what she could do with the common voice when she tried. Speech mistress gave her an award for the best cockney accent in Tunbridge Wells. Things changed at thirteen. Your father didn't know. Of course not. Her body let her down. And her little mind couldn't accept it. In my foolish way I softened life's blows. When she got engaged to that boy. I warned his family off. I clung to the belief it's so important for a girl to build a defence against the world. Instead of being so naked. Fighting it so unclothed. She used to ... When she was a baby. Something would spill. I'd go, "Why why why?" She's always say, "Cos cos cos, Mummy." I ... just don't think she can do it anymore.

TOUCHED   Stephen Lowe

*1945, right after VE Day in Europe and the end of World War II. A
working class home in Nottingham, North England. SANDRA (33)
is married to a British soldier posted overseas. SHE has become
pregnant by an Italian prisoner of war interned nearby. To the horror of HER family, SHE intends to have the baby. Here SHE recounts the inevitability of meeting the prisoner and HER attraction to
him.*

SANDRA: I took a picnic. What I could scrape together. Bread.
My ration of cheese. Flask of tea. I took it all nice. Lace tablecloth. I stood, looking through the barbed wire. I walked off when
they came out. Bent shouldered men in a crisp March. March.
March. I marched off at a good pace. He was right behind me.
Perhaps he spoke. I don't know. I had to find a certain place, that I
must have found before, but I was still surprised when we came
upon it. I must have found it earlier, but I couldn't believe it was
there, that I had looked for it, that I was returning to this place. I
thought the ground is hard and dry. It won't stain my tablecloth,
won't stain my dress. This is fine, anything can happen here, in the
lace of these trees, and it won't stain. I knelt, and began to unpack
my bag. I knew I could walk away and it may never have happened. I laid out the lace cloth, wiped out the creases, set out the
flask, the food, around the edges like for a child's party. I stood
and walked carefully around the outside of the edge. I looked up. I
faced him. We stood apart. It suddenly was a very hot day. I felt
faint. I thought, I'll fall. Look at him, I thought, look at him. He
began to speak. His voice rose. Anger? Hate? I couldn't understand what he was saying. The crispness was going. The fog was
setting in. His voice grew louder. He was undoing his clothing.
His trousers. I knew what he was saying. He was giving me orders. he was . . . giving me . . . orders. I looked at him, and I
knew the lace was there, the food was there. I looked at him. I

waited. Slowly his voice faded away. He stood there, unbuttoned, sad, clumsy against the lace, like a puppet with the strings broken. I spoke. I think they were the first words I spoke, and the last bar one. You—I pointed to him—PRISONER. He looked away. Frowned. Frowned like a little child. He understood me. It hurt me. NO. I said. I shook my head, meaning no. He looked up. I crossed the white to him. I put out my hand to him. I reached into his crumpled clothes, I touched him. Touched. I felt the shiver. The pulse. He is real. I . . . he . . . we are both here. The roughness of his clothes, the softness of the man's skin. I want to go down in front of him. I want him to go own in front of me. I want things I've never dreamed of, sins I have always feared. I pray. A second prayer. Not to ask, Lord, but to thank. I want to be free, and I am free. I am real. I am alive. The Lord is my shepherd. I shall not want. He maketh me to lie down in green pastures: he leadeth me beside the still waters. Thou preparest a table before me in the presence of thine enemies; my cup runneth over. Lord. Holy mother. Holy child. The Rainbow. The Rainbow.

TRUE DARE KISS   Debbie Horsfield

Spring 1980. A hairdressing salon in Manchester, England. BETH *(19), an unemployed but gregarious "punk" talks proudly to* HER *school friend,* NITA, *about* HER *attempt that day to enlist in the army. In the second monologue,* BETH, *on the street, comes in reading a newspaper that reports on a local disturbance.*

(BETH *marches on, salutes and stands to attention.*)
BETH: I did it.
[NITA *(putting the phone down)*: Did what?]
BETH: Volunteered. (NITA *looks blank*) The army.
[NITA *(as if she's heard it all before)*: Really?]
BETH: *(performing it)*: Information? Yeah, I come for informa-

tion. I come on a recce.

Committed? What's it look like? I'm here, aren't I?

Know what *I* done last week?—I'll show yer "committed"—y'know what? Seen *The Wild Geese* six times. Oh yeah, well there in't much *I* don't know about blowing people's balls off.

Question Number Two: Physical—right? Well cop this f'r'a specimen.

(SHE assumes a muscle-man pose) Rock hard, this is. *(Tapping HER stomach)* Solid rock.

I done two press-ups last week. Well not on the same day, obviously. Oh yeah, but ask us about marksmanship. Go on. Marksmanship? Now yer talking. I bin having a crack at me dad's air rifle . . . an' I'm getting pretty nifty. Oh yeah. Brought down —yesterday this is—brought down two japonicas an' an hanging basket. With one eye shut.

Yeah, right, okay—in traditional fields of armed warfare, what is the call—I know what yer sayin—for gunning down a fuchsia? Okay, okay, fair question. Let me finish. It's not the fuchsias, is it? It's the principle.

Have y'seen *The Wild Geese?* Y'should, honest. It's invaluable. The tactics . . . the manoevres . . . the right attitude . . . the right face. Like . . . what's this? *(SHE assumes a horrible face. Then as if it's obvious)* Roger Moore. *(SHE does another face, accompanied by a growl)* Richard Burton. Yeah. You *have* seen it, haven't yer?

Oh no, I'm not daft—I do know—*The Wild Geese* is mercenaries, right?—which is not *strictly* the same as army. Yeah, but it's all the same in the long run, in't it? Join the army, learn to be a bastard—then go out there an' put all that skill into practice. Get a few wars goin' . . . stage the odd coup. Y'could retire on yer winnings by the time yer forty. Also . . . and this is a point worth thinking about . . . mercenaries don't pay income tax. Well . . . yeah . . . that *is* usually 'cos they're dead . . . but what a way to go, eh?

[NITA: Beth . . . I don't know if you'd really be suited for the army.]

BETH: What d'y'mean?

[NITA: Bigoted . . . bad-tempered . . . loud-mouthed . . . aggressive . . . d'you want me to go on?]

BETH: Yeah, right, I know. I'm overqualified. So I'll just have to go in as a general.

* * *

(A street in Salford. BETH *comes in reading a newspaper.)*

BETH *(reading)*: "Situations Vacant". *(Looking through)* Sod-all, as usual. *(SHE turns to the front pages and reports of Moss Side riots)* Oh aye, the lads get a mention, do they? "Police Vehicle Set On Fire". Nice work boys.

(Folding the paper away) Me cousin lives across there. Our Sandy? Get told not to speak to her—her feller's a bit . . . y'know . . . *"Not all white"* But *I* do. Oh, *I* speak. Gets right up me dad's nose.

Her feller Paul—well, he should know, he says—he's got it back-to-back—her Paul says, gonna be bother soon. They gettin' bored playing silly buggers. Joy's gone out of mugging, robbing houses—where's the fun? Gettin' met by the muzzle of a bleedin' great bull terrier guarding empty cupboards full of dog food?

Sad state, innit?

Paul got the push down the soap factory. Wrong colour. *(SHE grins.)* Dun't look clean enough. Says, six months' time, be all dead quiet on the streets—all gone an' flogged the ghetto blasters, stop home an' booze theirselves to sleep. Get nasty round here, our Paul reckons. You watch, he says. Round here gonna go up soon.

"You lot", he says.

"Y'mean *me*?", I says.

"How come they let *you* unwind?

131

Build yer health clubs, saunas, leisure centres, three hundred quid members only Hard day's graft?—In the car—smash it out on court—down the golf course—prune the peonies—chammy the Porsche."

"Don't look at *me*," I says.

"See us?" he says. "Get home, hard day's hammer, no joy down the Job Centre—nobody lets *us* unwind."

"Fresh air," I says. "What more d'y'want?"

"Good enough fr'us," he says, "the waste tips, rubbish dumps, demolition sites. You lot," he says, "get narked, screw up, blow yer bottle?—that's legitimate. Show them yer fists?—They give yer a squash racquet. Us lot?—open hands—say please—go begging. No goals—so pick up the bricks."

It's called "Sport For All."

(Shouting:) Ta-ra, Al—goin' visitin' . . . *(As* SHE *goes)* Me cousins in Moss Side.

THE VAMPIRES   Harry Kondoleon

June, the present. The living room of CC *and* IAN's *elegantly furnished Victorian house. Late at night, after the couple have returned from a party.* CC *(35), wearing a black, strapless evening dress and a small, black cocktail hat with a thin, black feather pointing downwards, confronts* IAN *with the failure of their marriage. It seems the right time for* HER *to raise the subject.*

CC: I'm unhappy, I can't live this way, the way you are. Don't run away from me, Ian. We have problems, we should sit down and work them out. Don't ignore me, Ian. A drink isn't going to help—I know. Listen to me! Do you not love me anymore, Ian? Is that it? Say so then, that you don't need me or want me. Maybe we need a separation. If we need one let's have one then but tell me. Tell me we should have one. Talk to me! Where are you going—you're not going to bed! *(Ian exits upstairs)* Get back here! You have got to show me some consideration. Do you hear me? I thought you wanted to go to this ceremony. I didn't want to go. I thought it meant something to you. I broke my neck trying to finish this dress for tonight. You make fun of it in front of the first group of people we Meet—how am I supposed to interpret something like that, Ian? Am I supposed to take it as a joke? How can I? Come down here! Oh who am I kidding with this dress anyway?! *(While speaking SHE painstakingly removes the bottom part of the dress which has been pinned on. The seam isn't even sewn so, unpinned, it is a large, black, stiff piece of fabric. SHE is left with the top of the dress, panties, dark stockings and high-heeled shoes)* The invitation says black tie and half the people show up in dungarees and pullovers so I look like a Mardi gras float and then the editor of that coarse magazine you used to work for points out the pins in my dress as if she were uncovering a sex scandal! Ian! Ian! Are you coming down here? I'm trying to be understanding, Ian. I know you're going through a difficult career transaction period. Maybe some of your behavior these last few weeks has something to do with that actor's tragedy. That's not your fault, Ian, many actors get bad reviews, they just have to live with it, no one's to blame, you were just doing your job. But when you started laughing tonight during that woman's acceptance speech I was never so embarrassed in my entire life and you being one of the judges! But then I've lost count of most of the humiliations: you mimicking people at check-out counters, alienating each and every person we meet, contradicting me in front of my friends. I know I have very idealistic ideas about love but this marriage, Ian, is hitting some uncharted new low.

WHEN I WAS A GIRL I USED TO SCREAM
AND SHOUT . . .   Sharman Macdonald

1964. A beach in Scotland. VARI *(14 and 30s) moves back and forth between the present and past.* SHE *is played by the same actress in both cases. Here, as an adolescent,* SHE *describes to* HER *friend,* FIONA, HER *first sexual experience with a boy.* HER *description is quite graphic. In the second monologue, it is 1966.* MORAG *(42), the mother of sixteen-year-old* FIONA, *has just gotten out of* HER *bath. Never satisfied with* HER *daughter,* MORAG, *who divorced* HER *husband five years ago, uses this occasion to heap resentment onto* FIONA.

VARI: Anyway he kissed me. You know nice little nibbling ones not the great wet open-mouthed kind you get from some of them. Nice little nibbling things on the corner of my mouth and just down a bit. Then he puts his tongue in my mouth and that got a bit boring so I took his hand and put it on my breast. My right breast, I think it was. He seemed to like that though he didn't do much. Then that got a bit boring so I put my hand on his thing. Don't look like that. There comes a time when you've got to, you know, take things into your own hands. So I did. I mean I'd never seen one except on statues. Anyway tit for tat. He was groping away so why shouldn't I? It was all hard. I suppose I should have expected that but it was an awful shock. I sort of rubbed away a bit. Then he did it. He got it out. He undid his trousers and out it came. *(Pause)* It was very big. How does that ever fit into you? It was all sort of stretched and a bit purple. Though I couldn't see very well. It seemed rude to stop and stare. I mean if you've got something like that I don't suppose you really want it looked at. He didn't. Cause he got on top of me. He pushed me over. He pulled up my skirt. He stuck his fingers up inside my pants and inside me. Then he rubbed a bit, you know, himself up and down on me. Then he sort of gasped and stopped. There was this great wet patch on my skirt

134

when I got up. I told my mum I'd dropped my ice-cream, you know, old-fashioned vanilla. Say something. Go on. You think I'm dirty.

* * *

MORAG: *(Dressing)* I saw you when you were born. Two hours I was in labour with you and you ripped me right up to my bum. You came out from between my legs and your eyes were open. You knew exactly what you'd done. The midwife held you up. You looked right at me. You didn't cry. No, madam. Not you. You gave me look for look. I didn't like you then and I don't like you now. Do you hear me, Fiona? Are you listening, Fiona? I don't like you. Nasty little black thing you were. You had hair to your shoulders and two front teeth. You wouldn't suck. I tried to feed you. I did everything that was proper. You'd take nothing from me. Your father took you. He dandled you and petted you. You had eyes for him all right. Well, he's not here now. You won't find him down at the corner shop buying your sanitary towels. I took care of you. I clothed you and washed you and you had your fair share of cuddles. Sometimes I even quite liked you. Though you've gone your own way. You smoke, don't you? Don't you look at me like that. You walk back from that school every day, save the bus money for cigarettes. I know you do. I've seen you. I've not said. I've not said all I know about you. You sat on your father's knee, you clapped his head, you could get anything you wanted. You thought you could. You thought you could. You're still just a wee girl. Hanging round the prom on a Sunday teatime. I've seen you. Hanging round the boys. I've seen you, butter wouldn't melt in your mouth with your Sunday morning piety fresh on you and a smell of smoke on your breath. I've seen you looking at them. Sleekit smile on your face. You know it all. Well, do you, my girl? Do you know it all? You live in my house and in my house you do as I say and if anything happens to you with your sly ways you'll not stay in my house. You'll be out the door and you'll not come back. What you ask for you get. Now go and buy your sanitary towels.

(Silence)

I'm sorry. I love you. I'll always love you. I'm just out of the bath, Fiona. Are you asking me to catch my death?

WOMEN OF MANHATTAN

John Patrick Shanley

The present. Evening, after dinner, three women friends talk in the New York apartment of RHONDA LOUISE (28). SHE "hails from the Deep South, speaks and moves in a very deliberate way, and is slender and slow to react. HER frizzy, dark, brown hair frames a delicate, sensitive face. SHE is, by nature, always a trifle weary and a trifle solemn, or very weary and very solemn." RHONDA LOUISE tells HER girlfriends about how SHE threw out HER boyfriend and the aftermath of the break-up.

RHONDA: I didn't love him. Not in a way that led anywhere. I mean I loved him but it was like trying to hug a wall. How do you hug a wall? [. . .] I guess my big mistake was I revealed myself to him. That's where I really went wrong. You know, that thing that most people can't do? That thing that' supposed to be like the hardest thing to get to with another person? It took me time, but I struggled and strove and succeeded at last in revealing my innermost, my most personal soul to him [. . .] He just sat there with a coke in his hand like he was watching television, waiting for the next thing. Like that was a nice stop on the way to WHAT I CAN'T IMAGINE! The whole thing with him was such a letdown. But why am I surprised? You know? I mean, here I was congratulating myself on being able to show myself, show my naked self to a man. But what's the achievement? I chose to show myself to a wall.

Right? That's why I was able to do it. He was a wall an I was really alone, showing myself to nobody at all. How much courage does that take? Even when I got it together to throw him out, and I made this speech at him and got all pink in the face and noble as shit. He just said alright and left. What did I delude myself into thinking was going on between us if that's how he could take it ending? "Alright. Just lemme get my tools together, Rhonda Louise, and I'll get on to the next thing." You know how in that one school a thought you're the only thing real in the world, and everything else is just a dream? All these people and things, the stars in the sky, are just sparks and smoke from your own lonely fire in a big, big night. I always thought what a lotta intellectual nonsense that was until Jerry. I mean, to tell you the naked truth, I'm not even sure there was a Jerry. It seems impossible to me that there was. Sometimes I think I just got overheated, worked myself into a passion and fell in love with that wall right there. It must've been! It must've been that wall and me, crazy, loving it cause I needed to love. And not a human man. I couldn't have poured everything out to a really truly human man, and him just stand there, and take it, and give nothing back. It's not possible. But when I get too far gone in that direction of thinking—and alone here some nights I do—at those times it does me good to look and see these sneakers there sitting on the floor. His sneakers. He was here. It happened.

THE WORKROOM   Jean-Claude Grumberg
American version by Daniel A. Stein with Sara O'Connor

1947, after the war. A Tailoring workroom in Paris. SIMONE
(30s), a Jewish piece worker, speaks to another worker about HER
*husband, who was sent to a concentration camp during the war.
Uncertain whether he is dead or alive,* SHE *describes the hopeless
ordeal of trying to confirm his death and secure the proof of a death
certificate.*

SIMONE: They still won't give me the death certificate; a woman
told me she was told that a missing-person certificate was enough.
. . . But that depends . . . to get a pension it's not enough.
. . . They always make us fill out new papers; you never know
what your rights are. . . . No one knows anything. . . . They
toss us from one office to another. *(pause)* Because you've stood in
line everywhere, you end up knowing each other . . . ah the tall
stories go on and on. . . . There are some who always know
everything. . . . The mothers are the worst. . . . Did you have
to go through the Hotel Lutetia? *(He nods "yes")* They sent me there
at the very beginning to get information; someone who might have
seen him, who—you know what I mean. The photos, the—good.
I was only there once, I didn't dare go back. There was a woman
who grabbed me by the arm and shoved a photo in my face; the kind
they take on Awards Day. I can still see the little boy—he was the
same age as my eldest—in short pants, wearing a tie, clutching the
book he was given as the prize for excellence. She was screaming:
"He always got the prize for excellence." She didn't want to let go
of me; she kept repeating: "Why are you crying? Why are you
crying? Look, look, they're coming back—they'll *all* come back.
It's God's will. It's God's will." Then another woman shouted at
her and began to push her. . . . Someone ought to tell them
there's no hope for the children. Yet there they are, they keep
coming, they keep talking. . . . I've seen her time and again in the

138

offices, more and more crazy.... I spotted another one of them—his one never likes to stand in line; she always wants to be waited on first. Once I said to her: "You know, Madame, we're all in the same boat here; no need to elbow your way to the front. There's enough unhappiness for everyone ..." At the Prefecture, I met a Madame Levit, Levit with a "t" on the end. She was very nice, a good woman, but she was truly unlucky. Her husband was taken in '43, also, but he wasn't even Jewish, you see; his name was Levit, that's all.... She hasn't stopped running since. At first during the war it was to prove that he was—(SHE *searches for the exact word)*

[PRESSER: *(whispers)* Innocent?]

SIMONE: *(Nods "yes".)* And now, like us, she runs around just trying to find out what's become of him ... trying to get a little something.... She's a woman alone, with three children; she has no trade, she doesn't know how to do anything.... *(Silence. The* PRESSER *looks at* HER *without saying anything. Silence)* The hardest thing is not knowing ... thinking that perhaps he's lost somewhere, no longer able to remember even his name ... having forgotten me and the children. It happens ... it happens, but I tell myself that kind of illness cures itself with time.... The other day I was coming out of the market and I saw a man, with his back to me, holding a basket. I don't know why but I said to myself, just for a second, I thought: It's him! With a basket! It's funny because he wouldn't even go out to buy bread; he never ran errands. He didn't like to.... Anyway ... I mean you think of the times.... Here, I'm finished.... *(SHE hands him the piece. The* PRESSER *lights his lamp on the table and begins to iron it)* Anyway, if the Prefecture doesn't want to give out the death certificate it means they still have some hope; it means even they aren't sure of anything. Otherwise they'd be only too happy to make out all the papers and file all the records, so that everyone would be in order and no one would have to mention it anymore.

139

WRECKED EGGS   David Hare

*The present. Rhinebeck, New York, the pleasant living room of a
country retreat. GRACE (30s) is auburn-haired, with a light, hu-
morous voice, and a charming air of amusement. SHE has come to
stay with yuppie friends for the weekend. In the first monologue,
SHE refers to HER job as a press agent and what SHE has learned
about he meaning of success. In the second monologue, SHE talks
about one of HER clients, a real estate developer who is exploiting
property on Manhattan's Upper West Side and who wants a clean
image.*

GRACE: Reading about success is the new pornography. Look
I'll show you. *(SHE goes to search in a soft bag which SHE has
left, unpacked, near the door. From it she eventually removes a file)*
I keep this as a warning. If we had censors in this country and their
job was to cut every article which uses the word "survivor," if they
cut every word about *success*, if they cut every word about he rich
and their apartments, and what they eat, and what they sit on, and
what they have one their walls, and where they go in the summer,
and what other rich people they're sharing beds with, and why we
should envy them, and why we should think they are wonderful
people really, or in spite of it, or because of it, and how exactly they
made it, and why they made it and other people didn't, and what incredible pressure they have to put up with, and what a bore it is to
be recognized, and how difficult it is once you're successful to go
on being successful, if we cut every article which implies what's
successful must be good, if we just said sorry—press censor-
ship—this is Russia—none of that may appear . . . *(From the file
SHE removes a copy of the* Times.*)* Then this is the form in which
you would get your average morning paper. *(SHE holds it up. It is
like a conjuror's paper trick. So much has been cut from it that it
barely hangs together. It is just latticed shreds)*
[LOELIA: My God, look at it.]

140

(GRACE holds her hand up.)

GRACE: And now I shall read a copy of an average best-selling weekly magazine. *(SHE reaches into the bag. SHE moves towards the center of the room. SHE has nothing in HER hands. SHE mimes reading a non-existant magazine)*

[ROBBIE: Oh, I get it. It's nothing.]

GRACE: And once you know that's what it is, once you stop reading anything, *anything* which invites you to envy success, they you will find your daily reading material reduced to the back of cornflake boxes. *(SHE smiles and throws the shredded paper aside.)*

* * *

GRACE: No. I feel helpless. Don't you ever feel helpless? Like, at the moment my life is in real estate. I'm working for a developer. He's one of the most powerful men in New York. Tiny office,dark suits, forty. His wife, his oldest son, and his secretary. That's his whole staff. And from his two-room office, he's trying to tear down twelve blocks on the West Side of New York. *(SHE sweeps with her arm)* Docks are going to go. And houses. There's a park. There are shops. There are old apartment buildings. What we call *life*, in fact, that's what he's planning to remove. And in its place . . . you can imagine . . . you've seen it before he's even built it, it's dark, it's brutal, it's brown. It's eighty storeys of air-conditioned nothing. Great subdivided sections of air full of profit. For no conceivable human purpose at all.

(ROBBIE is about to interrupt, but GRACE anticipates)

All right, that's it, that's OK, let's say it's not even to be argued with. It's progress. He comes to *me*. He says, of course I hate personal publicity. I say, who doesn't? It's a given. It's why film stars ride in thirty-foot black limos—to be inconspicuous. It's why they have loud voices in restaurants, and employ people like me. Because they hate publicity so much. "What do you want," I said,

141

"a new image? People to like you? A positive slant on all this?"
"Oh no," he said "I just need a black fireball of controversy. That
way things will just burn themselves out." *(SHE leans forward)*
And he's *clever*, you see. He's not frightened. He understands the
process. We go for the cover of a New York magazine. "The
loathsome face of a property developer!" And inside it says "But he
gives money to charity." So he's what magazines call "complex".
He's got two sides to him. Well! He attends his children's school
play. And people eat this crap, they love it, it's called personality.
He's an asshole, *but*. What is he like? What is he like? is the only
question. The question is never "Is this right or wrong?" *(SHE
shakes her head, suddenly vehement)* It's not "Shall we do this?"
"Should this be done?" No, it's "Do we like the guy who's doing
this? Is he a nice guy?" Not even nice, is he good copy? Then,
hell, let him do what he wants. He wants a concentration camp for
millionaires on the West Side? Let him have it. He's an interesting
person. Forget the people who live on those blocks right now.
They have no personality. They'll never make the cover. So they
must be moved out of the way.

PLAY SOURCES

Anderson, Laurie. *New York Social Life.* In *United States.* New York: Harper & Row, 1984.

Barker, Howard. *Birth on a Hard Shoulder.* In *Two Plays for the Right.* London & New York: John Calder & Riverrun Press, 1982.

Beckett, Samuel. *Rockaby.* In *Rockaby and Other Short Pieces.* New York: Grove Press, 1981.

Berkman, Len. *Til the Beatles Reunite.* C/o The Author, Theatre Dept., Smith College, Northampton, MA 01063.

Berkoff, Steven. *Lunch.* In *West and Other Plays.* New York: Grove Press, 1985.

Cartwright, Jim. *Road.* London: Methuen, 1986.

Daniels, Sarah. *Ripen our Darkness.* London & New York: Methuen, 1986.

Dunn, Nell. *Steaming.* Oxford: Amber Lane Press, 1985.

Durang, Christopher. *The Marriage of Bette and Boo.* New York: Grove Press, 1987.

Fornes, Maria Irene. *The Conduct of Life.* In *Maria Irene Fornes: Plays.* New York: PAJ, 1986.

Fugard, Athol. *A Lesson From Aloes.* New York: Random House, 1982.

Glass, Joanna M. *Play Memory.* New York: Samuel French, 1984.

Glowacki, Janusz. *Hunting Cockroaches.* In *American Theatre,* May 1987, and *Formations Magazine,* Winter 1986-87, Vol. 3, No. 3.

Graczyk, Ed. *Come Back to the 5 & Dime Jimmy Dean, Jimmy Dean.* New York: Samuel French, 1984.

Grumberg, Jean-Claude. *The Workroom.* New York: Samuel French, 1984.

Hampton, Christopher. *Les Liasons Dangereuses.* London & Boston: Faber & Faber, 1986.

Hare, David. *Plenty.* New York: Penguin, 1978.

————. *Wrecked Eggs.* In *The Bay at Nice and Wrecked Eggs.* London & Boston: Faber & Faber, 1986.

Hastings, Michael. *Tom and Viv.* London: Penguin, 1985.

Heimel, Cynthia. *A Girl's Guide to Chaos.* C/o The American Place Theatre, 111 West 45 Street, New York 10036.

Henley, Beth. *Crimes of the Heart.* New York: Penguin, 1982.

Hoffman, William M. *As Is.* New York: Random House, 1985.

Horsfield, Debbie. *True Dare Kiss.* In *The Red Devils Trilogy.* London &

New York: Methuen, 1986.

Hwang, David Henry. *FOB*. In *New Plays USA 1*. New York: Theatre Communications Group, 1982.

Innaurato, Albert. *Passione*. New York: Dramatists Play Service, 1981.

Jacker, Corinne. *In Place*. New York: Dramatists Play Service, 1983.

_____. *Later*. New York: Dramatists Play Service, 1979.

Johnson, Charles R. *All Kidding Aside*. C/o the Author's Agent, Agency for the Performing Arts, 888 Seventh Avenue, New York, NY 10106.

Kazan, Nicholas. *Blood Moon*. New York: Samuel French, 1984.

Kempinski, Tom. *Duet for One*. New York: Samuel French, 1981.

Kesselman, Wendy. *My Sister in this House*. New York: Samuel French, 1982.

Kondoleon, Harry. *The Vampires*. New York: Dramatists Play Service, 1984.

LaGravenese, Richard. *Demigod*. In *A . . . My Name is Alice*. New York; Avon Books, 1985.

Lowe, Stephen. *Touched*. London & New York: Methuen, 1984.

Lucas, Craig. *Reckless*. New York: Dramatists Play Service, 1985.

Macdonald, Sharman. *When I Was a Girl I Used to Scream and Shout . . .* London: Faber & Faber, 1985.

Mack, Carol K. *Postcards*. New York: Samuel French, 1987.

Mann, Emily. *Still Life*. New York: Dramatists Play Service, 1982.

Mastrosimone, William. *Extremities*. New York: Samuel French, 1984.

_____. *Shivaree*. New York: Samuel French, 1984.

McLure, James. *The Day They Shot John Lennon*. New York: Dramatists Play Service, 1984.

Mueller, Lavonne. *Little Victories*. New York: Dramatists Play Service, 1984.

Noonan, John Ford. *All She Cares About Is the Yankees*. C/o The Author, 484 West 43 Street, 46G, New York, NY 10036.

Norman, Marsha. *'night, Mother*. New York: Hill & Wang, 1985.

O'Malley, Mary. *Once a Catholic*. New York: Samuel French, 1978.

Overmyer, Eric. *Hawker*. In *Short Pieces from the New Dramatists*. New York: Broadway Play Publishing, 1985.

Pielmeier, John. *Agnes of God*. New York: New American Library, 1985.

Rabe, David. *Hurlyburly*. New York: Grove Press, 1985.

Reddin, Keith. *Highest Standard of Living*. C/o The Author's Agent, Agency for the Performing Arts, 888 Seventh Avenue, New York, NY 10106.

Rimmer, David. *Album*. New York: Dramatists Play Service, 1981.

Robertson, Lanie. *Lady Day At Emerson's Bar and Grill*. C/o The Author's Agent, Helen Merrill, 361 West 17th Street, New York, NY 10011.

Saunders, James. *Bodies*. New York: Dramatists Play Service, 1979.

Selig, Paul. *Terminal Bar*. C/o The Author's Agent, Helen Merrill, 361 West 17 Street, New York, NY 10011.

Shange, Ntozake. *spell #7*. In *Nine Plays by Black Women*. New York: Mentor, 1986.

Shanley, John Patrick. *Danny and the Deep Blue Sea*. New York: Dramatists Play Service, 1984.

_____. *Women of Manhattan*. New York: Dramatists Play Service, 1986.

Shawn, Wallace. *Aunt Dan and Lemon*. New York: Grove Press, 1985.

Shepard, Sam. *Fool for Love*. New York: Bantam Books, 1984.

_____. *A Lie of the Mind*. New York: New American Library, 1986.

Simon, Neil. *Brighton Beach Memoirs*. New York: Random House, 1985.

Stoppard, Tom. *The Real Thing*. London and Boston: Faber and Faber, 1984.

Wagner, Jane. *The Search for Signs of Intelligent Life in the Universe*. New York: Harper & Row, 1986.

Weller, Michael. *Ghost on Fire*. New York: Grove Press, 1987.

Wendkos, Gina and Ellen Ratner. *Personality*. In *Women Heroes*. New York: Applause Theatre Book Publishers, 1987.

Wertenbaker, Timberlake. *The Grace of Mary Traverse*. London: Faber and Faber, 1985.

Whitemore, Hugh. *Stevie*. Oxford: Amber Lane Press, 1984.

Wilson, August. *Fences*. New York: New American Library, 1986.

_____. *Ma Rainey's Black Bottom*. New York: New American Library, 1985.

Wolfe, George C. *The Colored Museum*. New York: Broadway Play Publishing, 1987.

* * * * *

Many of the above published titles are available by mail in major theatrical bookshops across the country. All titles are available and may be ordered through APPLAUSE THEATRE BOOKS, 211 West 71 Street, New York, NY 10023. Send $4 for a complete catalog. Or call (212) 595-4735.

ONE ON ONE

BEST MONOLOGUES FOR THE 90'S
Edited by Jack Temchin

You have finally met your match in Jack Temchin's new collection, **One on One**. Somewhere among the 150 monologues Temchin has recruited, a voice may beckon to you—strange and alluring—waiting for your own voice to give it presence on stage.

"The sadtruth about most monologue books," says Temchin. "is that they don't give actors enough credit. I've compiled my book for serious actors with a passionate appetite for the unknown."

Among the selections:
David Mamer OLEANNA
Richard Greenberg THE AMERICAN PLAN
Brian Friel DANCING AT LUGHNASA
John Patrick Shanley THE BIG FUNK
Terrence McNally LIPS TOGETHER, TEETH APART
Neil SimonLOST IN YONKERS
David Hirson LA BETE
Herb Gardner CONVERSATIONS
WITH MY FATHER
Ariel Dorfman DEATH AND THE MAIDEN
Alan Ayckborn A SMALL FAMILY BUSINESS

$7.95•paper
MEN: ISBN 1-55783-151-3•WOMEN: ISBN: 1-55783152-1